THE GUIDEBOOK TO AUTHENTIC SUCCESS

BEYOND THE MEASURE OF MONEY

CARL MASSY

BOOKS IN 'THE GUIDEBOOK SERIES'

The Guidebook to Happiness
The Guidebook to Optimum Health
The Guidebook to Authentic Success

Copyright © 2017 by Carl Massy. All rights reserved, including the right to reproduce this book or portions of it in any form whatsoever, or stored in a database or retrieval system, except in the case of brief quotations embodied in critical articles and reviews.

First printed in 2017.
Cover design and book layout by Ferry Tan of Invisible Resources.

For information about special discounts for bulk purchases, please contact Carl Massy at: carl@carlmassy.com.

For information about bringing Carl Massy or his team to a live event or delivering an in-depth transformational workshop, please contact Carl Massy at:
carl@carlmassy.com.

DEDICATION

To my amazing partner, Ferry, who is still here after book three. Talk about dedication! You make me and my life so much richer. Thank you.

To all of the amazing teachers, past and present, I have had the privilege to learn from and share experiences with — thank you for sharing your wisdom. And to every person I have had the privilege to work with, you help me to learn and grow.

CONTENTS

Chapter 1:

Introduction 9

Chapter 2:

Authentic Success 17

Chapter 3:

The Authentic Success Pillars 21

Chapter 4:

Visioning Success 31

Chapter 5:

The Importance of Passion 37

Chapter 6:

Potential, Meaning and Choices 41

Chapter 7:

Power Versus Force 47

Chapter 8:

Your Personal Authentic Success Audit   53

PART 1: MINDSET   57

Chapter 9:

An Introduction to Mindset   59

Chapter 10:

Beliefs & Stories   63

Chapter 11:

On Identity   71

Chapter 12:

Thinking Patterns   77

Chapter 13:

Consciousness   83

PART 2: STRATEGIES 97

Chapter 14:

An Introduction to Strategies 99

Chapter 15:

Daily Positive Emotions 103

Chapter 16:

High Quality Relationships 115

Chapter 17:

Feeling Connected 125

Chapter 18:

Growing 133

Chapter 19:

Living a Life of Purpose 139

Chapter 20:

Getting into Financial Flow 147

Chapter 21:

Alignment with Authentic Self 159

PART 3: HEALTH AND VITALITY — 167

Chapter 22:

An Introduction to Health and Vitality — 169

Chapter 23:

The 6 Pillars to Optimum Health and Vitality — 173

Chapter 24:

Lifestyle Habits — 185

PART 4: BONUS STRATEGIES — 197

Chapter 25:

Strategies to Serve You — 199

Chapter 26:

Honing Your Decision-Making Skills — 209

Chapter 27:

Conclusion — 217

Chapter 28:

Recommended Resources — 221

Chapter 29:

Recommended Reading — 225

Acknowledgements — 229

CHAPTER 1
Introduction

For those of you who have read *The Guidebook to Happiness* or *The Guidebook to Optimum Health*, I welcome you back and truly thank for joining me again as your part-time guide.

These days I deliver numerous presentations, workshops and seminars, and when I ask people in the audience to put up their hand if they would like to be more successful, there's not a hand in the audience that remains down. Everyone wants to be more successful. But what does being successful mean for each of us?

What does being successful mean to you?

I ask all of my coaching clients this and all too often the default answer is income—the amount of numbers on your their paycheck. But is the person who earns $50,000 a month but spends more than they earn successful? Are they happy?

In our slightly materialistic world (yes, I'm being sarcastic), there is an unhealthy focus on fame, power, beauty and financial wealth as the determinants of modern-day success. We think, "When I have money then I will be fulfilled and content." Hmmm. Sorry, but that may not actually be the case. Positive psychology and social psychology therapists suggest that the happiest people are those who have better relationships and better health and that happiness actually comes *before* success and a higher income as opposed to the other way around.

Most of us have been conditioned by society to see success looking a particular way. We've been lead to focus our attention (and our game plan) on LOOKING successful, which means having all the toys of success—the hot cars, the swimming pool, the Rolex watch. And if someone picks up a book on success, they expect to read about how to make a business work, or how to make a killing in the market, or become an expert in their chosen field so they can make more money and get those things. But listen, I've worked with clients that are multimillionaires who still have a scarcity mindset. I can assure you the money thing is a piece of the pie. But it's not the whole pie.

I want more than that for you. I actually want a LOT more than that for you. The desire I have is for you to FEEL successful. There's an enormous difference between looking successful and feeling successful. And I want to assist you with not just being and looking successful, but feeling deeply successful and fulfilled in your entire body.

Are you ready for that kind of success?

A little background

Those returning will be familiar with my background story becoming a strategic planning expert and personal development and health coach (except this time around I'm telling it from the perspective of success). So please bear with a little repetition in this introduction while I get everybody else up to speed.

My working life started at the tender age of 17 when I stepped a tentative foot into the Australian Defence Force Academy as an Army

Officer Cadet. We'd made it through a grueling selection process with thousands of other applicants from all over Australia, and were told by the Academy we constituted the top five percent of talent in the country. I was sure I was already successful! From that point onwards I had a strong success mentality.

By the time I was 34 I was working as a senior security consultant to the Athens 2004 Olympic Games, living in downtown Athens in an awesome apartment (party pad). My income had more than doubled since I left the Australian Army as a major. I was provided with a car, plenty of annual leave, and rarely worked more than 40 hours per week. I was part of an elite team in a specialist role of explosives management. (Bomb defence to health coach? Go figure!)

I definitely looked successful.

Thing is, I was not taking good care of my health. As you can imagine, work conditions were emotionally stressful. And yet I and my team were taken for granted and there was little emotional reward. I felt disconnected from myself and my bigger purpose. As a result I ended up with pneumonia, followed by pleurisy—an infection of the lining of the lungs that makes you feel like you've been sucker punched in the ribs by Mike Tyson. At that point I was definitely not feeling too successful.

The great thing about adversity is it causes us to wake up and pay attention to what is and isn't working in our lives. At that point I decided to reevaluate what what success meant to me and what I wanted my path to success to look like. I also started to hatch a plan to finally do what I'd always wanted to do: Inspire people – not freak them out by telling them stories about bombs exploding and showing them horrific graphic slideshows.

A seed had actually been planted in 1999 when I attended a seminar by Anthony Robbins, and saw what a success coach was all about. I got charged up about helping people experience more joy by becoming the best version of themselves, whether that was physically, mentally, or emotionally. But first I had to do it for myself. As I reassessed my life, I rapidly moved away from defining success in terms of money and my party pad to doing what made me happy. Which was a huge step. But I still hadn't defined what being successful actually *meant* for me.

It's only been in recent years, after the inevitable highs and lows of life matured me, that I've taken a closer look at what success actually means ... what leads to a FEELING of success. How it's possible to *feel* successful in my bones. How it's possible to experience success at the cellular level and in all the different areas of life.

As I studied success more thoroughly I found an amazing thing happened when I put the word 'authentic' in front of the word: It changed the tone and depth of the conversation. Suddenly the theme of success started expanding sideways into other aspects of life. It touched on relationships and health and whether we're making a meaningful difference in the world. It made success about *me*.

One of my favourite quotes is by Earl Nightingale, writer, speaker, author and advocate of human character development back in the 1950's. He said, "*Success is the progressive realization of a worthy ideal.*"

I love this quote and use it often because it's short and easy to remember and because the focus on a "worthy ideal" is what breathes meaning and depth into life. It also reveals the fact that you can feel successful as soon as you *start moving in the direction of something you have deemed to be worthy and meaningful*. You can feel successful before you arrive at your destination—*if* you choose a meaningful goal and stay the course.

Authentically feeling successful before material success even occurs? Wow! That's huge!

It's been a long journey for me getting beyond the superficial trappings of success into the heart of what success is really all about. And I've been really excited to share this information with you.

Do I consider myself to be successful today? By my own terms of success (the only terms that matter which you will learn for yourself!), I can say, "Yes." I run a successful coaching business. I'm an owner in a successful yoga centre in Bali called *The Practice*, which is focused on helping people to become healthier, happier, more joyful and more successful by using yoga and its teachings as a tool. I have an amazing, loving and joyful relationship which I have been in for more than eight years. My health is fantastic and I look younger than my chronological age (I think I look 10 years younger, but it might be closer to 9 ;-) I have more vitality than a lot of people 20 years younger.

Am I a bazillionaire? No. Do I want to be? No. Would I like to increase my net worth? Yes. Would that allow me to do more meaningful things for others and myself? (My worthy ideal) Yes! Am I human? Yes! There are definitely some days I feel more successful than others. And there are some areas in which I feel more successful than others. I'm not about to stand on a pedestal and tell you I have it all figured out all the time and have the perfect life. That would be total BS. And if anyone else tries to present that image you can be certain they are full of it too.

What I am certain about is that I can show you specific tips, tools and strategies that will have you feeling even more successful right down to your bones, and provide you with a useful roadmap to guide you along the path of your worthy ideal for the rest of your life.

Is this a book about how to get rich in 30 days? Hell no. I don't want you being the richest unhappy person on the block. I want you to be the most wealthy, healthy, fulfilled and joyful person on the block. This will definitely make you more fun to hang out with and, at the same time, make the world an even nicer place to be.

Am I going to give you tips on how to increase your income? You bet. Over the course of this book you'll discover the tools and strategies that will trigger a feeling of deep success in your life. You'll learn what else besides money is required for being and feeling successful. You'll learn what is missing in your life, keeping you from success. You'll be guided to find other means than pure cashola to experience the feeling of success in a meaningful way. And I will assist you in discovering your worthy ideal.

The structure of this book

This book is presented in 4 Parts and has two different interlaced frameworks. The first framework is one I use in coaching programs to help clients experience success in their lives. It looks like this:

1. A clear vision
2. The right mindset
3. Effective strategies
4. Available energy and vitality

The second framework, which is specifically relevant to the subject of this book, are the 8 pillars for achieving authentic success.

Part 1 helps you establish a clear vision and ensures that you have the right mindset to achieve the highest level of success possible. Part 2 explores the first seven of the 8 pillars of authentic success. Part 3 presents the 8th pillar: Optimum Health and Vitality. And finally Part 4 gives you Bonus Strategies that will make a difference in the quality of the decisions you make and the results that you get.

Ready to get started? Great! I'm SUPER grateful to be your guide through this book. I not only look forward to providing you practical and applicable strategies, but I also hope to entertain you along the way because remember: The greatest learning is achieved with a light heart.

CHAPTER 2
Authentic Success

Let's get clearer about what I mean when I say "success." Then we'll get into *authentic* success which is where the sweet spot is. Here's a scenario based on a previous client of mine—a great woman who happened to be a lawyer.

Dorothy (or so I'll call her) worked for a large firm for a number of years and then teamed up with a colleague to start her own law practice. Working in a small practice, she had autonomy and a lot more input into what clients and specific cases she took on. She had the prestige of owning her own business. She earned very good money and it allowed her to live in a nice apartment, to experience international travel (both business and personal), and to buy all the physical possessions she wanted.

Was she successful? From external appearances, it would appear that she was quite successful.

But when she came to me for coaching and I asked her, "Are you happy?" that's when I started to see more of the actual picture and a few cracks started to show. Turns out everything looked good on the surface. But she wasn't happy all the way through. She was successful in some areas but not successful overall. Which brings me to my point about authenticity.

Authentic success is holistic. It's supportive of the whole. It requires us to address a number of different areas if we want to not only feel successful, but also feel happiness, joy, and a healthy flourishing sense of ourselves.

Authentic success is long-term, not a fleeting moment. It's dependent upon more than one or two factors. Most of all, authentic success is about being unapologetically, unequivocally and unashamedly yourself in a "down to the bones" sort of way. As it turns out, Dorothy was trapped in a classic "imposter syndrome," putting a mask on every day to earn her success—something you may have experienced at some level yourself.

She not only had to wear a suit to work everyday, she also had to wear a metaphorical suit as well. She had to go from being this caring, creative, intelligent, attractive woman to being a hard-arsed lawyer mixing it up with the guys. She couldn't show up as the beautiful woman that she was in fear of sending the wrong signals.

Which means she wasn't *authentically* successful at all.

As I've said, success is more than a healthy financial balance sheet. Sure, there's a bunch of research that suggests that money is a factor in our happiness up to a certain level. And I'm all for having money. But as Martin Seligman, one of the founders of Positive Psychology, suggests in his updated framework on what leads to an individual flourishing, the quality of our relationships has a major impact on whether or not we flourish—*especially our relationship with ourselves*.

Now, for those of you who'd like a little more (or lot more) cash lining your pockets, don't think I've gone all hippie on you. Money is DEFINITELY part of the whole success thing and it can greatly serve you—as long as you aren't serving *it*.

But honestly, I've found that it's less about the amount of money you have and more about the belief you have in your ability to generate more when you need it that counts. A person may have millions but still feel financially *insecure* (which is a whole other topic). Whereas a person may have $5,000 in the bank and feel good as gold because they have a strong belief, supported by personal experience, that they can generate more cashola if they need to.

Which begs the question: Who is actually more successful in this case?

CHAPTER 3
The Authentic Success Pillars

I'd like to share with you the key pieces that make up the authentic success picture—where the feeling of success is not just skin deep but saturates every cell in your body.

The pillars are not listed in order of priority order—they ALL matter. And I'm also not arrogant enough to think the list I'm presenting is the Eight Commandments to Success, chiseled in granite and eternally written. After working with a diverse range of clients over the years I've realized everybody's definition of success and value structures vary. However there are some common factors that lead to a deeper experience of success and seem apply to just about everybody. These are:

1. Daily joy
2. High-quality relationships
3. Feeling connected
4. Growing/evolving
5. Meaningful life goals
6. Financial flow
7. Being aligned with authentic self
8. Optimum health & vitality

It's my experience that it's difficult to feel deeply successful if you sacrifice any of these key pieces. That said, please know the importance of each item will vary from individual to individual. Different people will be stronger in different areas going into the process of creating authentic success. Life is an OPPORTUNITY for learning and growth. And part of the process of growth is figuring out the things that need more attention in our lives, what we need to work on more, redefine and refine, and perhaps get help with.

Now let's look at each item in more detail.

1. Daily positive emotions (aka: Daily Joy)

Joy represents a range and cocktail of feelings that come under the positive emotions umbrella. The word is pretty joyful to say. It's got a sweet taste.

Joy is not about planting a silly grin on your face. It's a feeling of wellbeing, excitement and love for life that wells up in your body, automatically bringing a smile to your face. You feel great just to be alive.

Are you truly successful if you don't experience joy on a regular basis? (And when I say a regular basis I mean daily.) What about if your your daily level of joy rates a seven out of a possible ten. Are you successful?

2. High-quality relationships

Are you successful if you don't have high-quality relationships with your intimate partner, children, family, business associates, and friends?

And what do I mean by a high-quality relationship?

A great relationship with somebody means you feel better about yourself after you spend time with them. You feel more energized as opposed to feeling more drained. Great relationships cause you to grow. They allow you to become an even bigger and better version of yourself. Great relationships provide you with a sense of safety and security so you feel confident to stretch yourself, take chances, and lean into uncertainty knowing you have support if things end up looking more like a disaster movie than a bed of roses.

Great relationships bring out your best. They challenge you to be authentic, to show up as yourself and feel free doing so without judgment. A great relationship also means you can count on the other person to call you on your crap if you're a being a lightweight, insensitive, phony, etcetera.

High-quality relationships have nothing to do with having thousands of "friends" on Facebook or getting a lot of likes or hearts on the posts you make on your social media sites. A key trait to high-quality relationships is DEPTH. Remember we're not here to settle for superficial success. We're after the stuff that's authentic and rests deep in our core.

3. Feeling connected

Are you successful if you feel disconnected from yourself? From other people? From the environment? From your work or calling and from life in general? I would say not.

Yes, this borders on being a spiritual thing. But feeling as if we're an integral part of life as it unfolds around us is really vital to our sense of stability and wellbeing. Feeling we're part of something bigger, feeling that the universe, life, God, Allah or whatever you want to call it, is *for you* and not against you gives us tremendous security.

For the guys reading this, I want you to hang onto your seats now and go with me on this one. (Consider it prep for when I get to the "L" word, which I will in a minute.) Connection is about feeling accepted and worthy of being on the planet. It's about feeling accepted for being your imperfect perfect self—the one who makes mistakes, is inappropriate at times, offends people on a regular basis (that would be me), who reacts with the intelligence of a dog in certain social circumstances, who is crap at some skill that everyone else has apparently mastered, and a host of other very human qualities. Connection is about you accepting, approving and loving who you are—you being connected to you and connected to this joyous thing called life.

4. Growing

Are you truly successful if you don't feel like you're evolving? If you don't feel like you're stretching yourself and becoming greater? I know my answer. What's yours?

I don't mean to be melodramatic here, but do you know what's happening when a plant stops growing? It's on its way to dying. Tony Robbins—that 6'7" success coach and successful author from the USA who's worked with thousands and thousands of people in his 40-year career—has formulated a list of basic human needs which are: Certainty, uncertainty, significance, love & connection, contribution, and GROWTH.

It's very hard for someone to feel fulfilled in life if they don't have a sense of growth. Just as the universe is growing and expanding, we, too, have an inbuilt need to be expanding, whether it's physically, emotionally, mentally, or spiritually. I've worked with a number of couples over the years, and when their relationship stops growing and they as individuals stop evolving, the relationship is definitely in trouble. Unless they bring more challenge and growth into the relationship it will stagnate even more, become an arduous chore, or burst apart at the seams.

5. Meaningful life goals (making a difference)

When I teach about goals, goal setting, and getting clear on your vision, I take everyone through a mini checklist—a quick three criteria test (which I learnt from some other smart person) to determine the meaningfulness of someone's goals. I ask them:

1. **Is the goal good for you?** Does it make you a better person in a healthy, non-narcissistic way that contributes to your life experience? That helps you evolve and become even more? Is your goal something that brings out the best version of yourself?

2. **Is the goal good for others?** Is your goal good for the people around you? It's not very healthy striving for a goal that negatively impacts your family and friends in a major way. A meaningful goal needs to be worth what it will take to get. And losing your friends, partner and family along the way is definitely not a part of the success formula. Although we've all seen people do it, this is not something I wish for you. I want you to flourish. So do ask this question and pay close attention to what feedback you get.

3. **Is the goal positive for the greater good?** When I say greater good I'm talking about things like the environment, your community, or the planet. Is it going to have a positive impact and make a difference in peoples' lives? Are you going to leave the planet in a better state then before you came along? This doesn't mean you

have to be a Gandhi or a Mother Teresa. Goals that are healthy for the greater good can mean raising two amazing children, or being an outstanding role model in your community, or teaching your life lessons to disadvantaged youths.

Basically we humans have an inherent need to contribute beyond ourselves—what you might also call "making a difference." The more we can make the attainment of our goals positively impactful for others, the better we feel about ourselves and the more authentically successful we feel.

6. Financial flow

What I have to learn about the money scenario is, it's not so much about the amount of money we have, but the feeling and beliefs we have about our ability to generate more when we need it that count. Which translates into the feeling of genuine CONTROL over our financial situation.

I've worked with clients who thought they needed more money to feel financially secure, when the reality was having more money just meant they were a more wealthy insecure person. What's the good of that?

Perhaps the ideal mix contributing to a feeling of success around money is having an amount of savings for unforeseen situations, a regular flow of money that allows us to have the lifestyle that is most desirable for us, and then an unerring belief in our ability to generate money if and when we need it.

Despite social belief to the contrary, having a huge desire for a lot of money isn't even healthy. In his book *Why We Do What We Do*, Edward Deci, a professor of psychology and social sciences, says "Researchers found that having an unusually strong aspiration for material success was associated with narcissism, anxiety, depression, and poorer social functioning as rated by a trained clinical psychologist."

Financial flow isn't about wealth accumulation. It's about letting money be the *by-product* of doing what you love in a way that brings you joy, connects you with amazing people, helps you grow, makes a positive difference, allows you to stay true to yourself, and maintains your health. If lots of money is your central focus at the expense of these other pieces, you might feel financially rich. But you are unlikely to feel fulfilled and jazzed .

Life is what's it's all about. And that's a much bigger game than having bucket loads of bucks.

7. Aligned with authentic self

Are you successful if your heart's not in the game? If you're constantly looking over the fence at the other people having a good time, wondering why you're doing what you're doing? Are you successful if you have to put on a mask every day to show up at work or show up in your relationship?

There's a good reason that the best actors get paid the big bucks. It's bloody hard work and a real energy drain pulling off being someone other than who you are.

The purpose of our lives on planet Earth is to fully express our **authentic and unique self** in ways that serve us and others. My most rewarding work as a coach and teacher is to help people truly express who and what they are—to let their individual gifts shine—to step into the biggest version of their authentic self—to bring the dream they have burning in their chest into the light of day.

In my experience it's very hard to feel successful if we're not being true to who we are and what we have to offer. Suppress yourself and you're suppressing life and a remarkable gift for humanity.

Are you showing up with integrity? Do you like yourself? Do you like how you are and how you interact with the world? Do you walk the talk? Are you in alignment with what you know to be right and good for yourself and the people around you?

Living a life of integrity aligned with you you really are is not about being perfect or perceived as perfect. We all make mistakes. We say and do the wrong things on occasion. We hurt others by accident. We fail at a goal we've set ourselves. That's just life. Integrity is being true to ourselves, knowing we're doing our best as much as possible.

Who could ask for anything more?

8. Optimum health and vitality

Is someone successful if they have millions of dollars but their body is giving out on them? If they re sick and feel like crap, have no energy to do anything and look ten years older than they are? Of course not! Remember the old saw about the man who sacrificed his health to create wealth then spent his wealth in a desperate attempt to recover his health?

How about playing the game of life a little more strategically and consciously?

If you know anything about me, you know I'm extremely passionate about health and vitality. My second book was called *The Guidebook to Optimum Health* for a good reason. I believe it's difficult to get the most out of life or become the best we can be if we don't have the vitality and health to go the distance. What good is having lots of money if you don't have the energy and health to fully utilise it?

We all know people who've let their health suffer and their body go pear shaped who don't feel good about themselves at all. It's hard to feel truly successful if you don't love the person you see in the mirror.

CHAPTER 4
Visioning Success

Vision

What does success look like to you? Feel like and sound like to you? If we don't get clear about what we're aiming for, we're less likely to know in which direction to head or what changes we need to make along the way.

As we go through this book, I'm going to ask you to picture what success would look like for you from the perspective of each of the 8 Authentic Success Pillars. And there are several good reasons why I want you to come up with this clear overall vision.

First off, what if you're already successful and don't even know it? It's totally possible. Maybe you've been looking at your life from someone else's point of view and definition of success. Your father's? Your mother's? Your partner's? Some savvy marketer convincing you that you're incomplete and unsuccessful until you have their product or service? ;-) I've seen quite a few people get clear on what success means to them and suddenly realise they were already standing right in the middle of it.

The second reason I want you to create a clear vision is because you must if you're going to take the level of success you're currently experiencing to a whole new level. And not just the next level on the ladder. I'm talking a whole new level entirely—a Star Trek quantum leap reappearing in a whole new arena of success entirely. How would that feel? Pretty damn fine I am guessing.

The third reason is I want you to experience real change—right down to the cellular level. I want you to experience lasting change that doesn't fade away. And to do that you have to actually rewire your brain for success.

The brain 101

Your brain is amazing. It's never turned off. Even when you sleep at night, your brain is still processing memories, regenerating cells, rejuvenating systems, cleaning, cleansing, eliminating, and several trillions of other things, all at the same time. Best of all, everything is happening automatically. You don't have to do any thinking to make this happen.

Everything you've learned and experienced in the past determines the way your brain is wired (meaning how the neurons actually hook up in associative patterns that help you to function). Your brain and its neuronal wiring is also affected by your genetics—which is basically all the learned experience from human history stored in your DNA. (More of the *past* stuff).

The bit called our "mind" or "consciousness" is tougher to grasp. Some biologists would say the mind is a result of complex chemical and electrical processes in the brain. Other scientists would say consciousness impacts the workings of the brain creating "mind thoughts." I lean towards the second hypothesis. I believe our consciousness can impact the physiology of the brain. Take for instance studies on long-term meditators who apply their consciousness in such a way that they change the physical structure of their left prefrontal lobe—an area neuroscientists associate with wellbeing. In this case the mind impacted the physicality of the brain.

So, if your consciousness and the things you think about can effectively rewire the brain, consider what happens when you imagine things you haven't yet experienced, learned or even seen.

The reason it's so IMPORTANT that we spend time, energy and effort to form a CLEAR VISION of what we want in our lives is because the new images can actually change the inner workings of your brain. Which means your vision of success—when you walk into it—will be permanent (unless you un-vision it). You'll literally be rewired for greater success instead of forever playing out old scripts from the past.

How do you optimize your brain so you can become even more successful in all areas of your life? Read on.

Employing the RAS 24/7

Sounds like a cool electronic gadget doesn't it? But no. RAS stands for *reticular activating system* (or *extrathalamic control modulatory system* if you want to impress people at the next geek party you attend). It's located in the brain region referred to as the mammalian brain or mid-brain. It's located in a space that connects it to the upper-brain called the cortex and the lower brain called the cerebellum, which manages the nervous system.

One of the most important roles of the RAS is to act as a filter for sensory information being passed into our conscious mind. There are millions of bits of sensory information being picked up every second via all our senses, and our conscious mind only has the ability to process a fraction of these. It's the role of the reticular activating system to filter sensory information.

Now the RAS can either filter the sensory information based on our past beliefs or it can filter sensory information relating to what we choose to imagine and consciously focus upon. If we want to create our destiny and future success it helps to program the RAS in a process called "priming." In other words, we want the RAS to be hypersensitive to sensory inputs that support our specific vision. We want our powerful brains, via the RAS and our sensory receptors, to be on the lookout for the opportunities, people, resources, ideas, strategies, insights, and situations that align with our main vision and key desires.

Here's an example of priming. Say you've been looking long and hard for the perfect cool car—one that will stand out from the crowd. Cruising the car dealerships you finally find the perfect car in a very unique color and style you've never seen before, and you part with a wad of cash. You drive on your merry way with a broad smile on your face thinking you and the car are SO special.

But then the unthinkable happens. You're hardly two blocks from the car dealership and you spot another car exactly like yours! It even has the same color trim. By the time you get home you're distraught because you saw another three cars the same as yours on the 30-minute ride home!! How could this happen?!?!

Unfortunately for you and your new coolness, turns out there were ALWAYS these other cars on the road. You didn't notice them because you weren't primed to do so. Your RAS didn't know to be on the lookout for a particular make and model of car because you hadn't see it yet. But when you took ownership of your new car you suddenly had a clear and emotionally charged image playing out repeatedly in your mind. Your

RAS was *primed* to notice other cars that fit that image.

The awesome thing about the RAS is that it can be primed by your conscious mind with any image you want. As Tony Robbins says, "The past does not equal the future." Regardless of past results or experience or upbringing or emotional abuse by your jealous sibling, you get to CHOOSE what you want your powerful brain and mind to focus on. Your amazing brain will know *exactly* what to look out for as it sifts through millions of bits of sensory information.

And don't think you're limited to RAS priming and your five standard senses of sight, sound, touch, taste and smell to help you towards your goal. Quantum physics tells us we're all connected to everything at the quantum level of energy. Which means you're already hooked up to all the things you need to bring your vision of success into reality. You just needed to send out the right, clear message.

Things like intuition, insight, and gut feelings are very real. They're a different kind of data input that will take you closer to what you desire. And if, by chance, you're skeptical of "unseen" forces, let me ask you this: Have you ever been thinking of someone you've not thought of in months and suddenly they pop up in your life? They call or instant message or even show up on your doorstep? And you say, "That's weird, I was just thinking of you…"

I am yet to meet anyone who hasn't experienced this at least once in their lives. For many of us this is a regular occurrence. So not only can RAS priming and creative visualization help you at the regular physical level, your visualization and intent also set quantum dynamics in motion, drawing you towards your goals and the objects of your desire towards you.

Throughout the rest of this book covering the 8 Pillars of Authentic

Success I'll be prompting you to get very good at planting a clear and emotionally-charged vision in your mind of *what you really want*. Then let your RAS and quantum processes go to work for you.

CHAPTER 5
The Importance of Passion

If you have children you've *definitely* heard the words, "But why?" Usually delivered in a whiney tone of voice. As a kid I was pretty hyperactive. (Actually not much has changed on that front.) Which means I wasn't a fan of sitting still for long. Which means long car drives were painful for the whole family unless the reason for the drive was revealed up front.

It's amazing how fast you can park your arse in the back seat of a car when the proposed long drive ends with a visit to SeaWorld at the Gold Coast in Australia. I could go from zero to 10 in a matter of seconds on the promise of some future possibility that appealed to me. Just the thought—the picture in my mind of riding the waves and watching the dolphin show—caused a cascade of emotions rushing through my body, propelling me into action.

My point is this: If we want to become motivated to act, we need to fire up our emotions. There's a common saying in the coaching field: "Emotion creates motion." And it does. Directed, strategic actions take us closer to our goals and the experience of authentic success. But it's our emotions that kick our actions into gear.

And what kicks our emotions into gear? Our thoughts.

The more powerful your thoughts, the greater the emotional response, the more motivated and inspired you are to act. I realize I haven't gotten into this yet, but it's important to know at this point that our thoughts initiate a neurological and biochemical response in our brains that immediately sets off a cascade of responses through our bodies. With every thought, neuropeptides, neurotransmitters and hormones are released into the bloodstream, causing the systems in our body to shift into action. The more powerful and emotional the thought, the greater the release of biochemicals in the body.

We'll explore the link between thoughts and emotions more when we look into the subject of mindsets, but I wanted to introduce the idea here. On the way to the fulfillment of our greatest desires, we inevitably face obstacles. The greater the REASONS we have for doing something, the more inspired and motivated we become, the more effectively our bodies will respond and overcome any resistance.

Do ya really want it?

Who do you think is more likely to put in the effort and remain persistent to the attainment of their goal out of the following two people: 1) the person who has a great intellectual idea to create a particular product, or 2) the person who wants to create a similar product but has a burning desire in their heart to do it?

One of the top criteria for success is passion. We absolutely need emotional engagement if we want to get something important done. Having our head in the game is not enough. Success is greatly enhanced by being masterful at managing and utilizing our emotional states.

Which means one of the key criteria to success and achieving your individual goals is the power of your WHY.

What are the reasons you want to achieve a particular goal? I never let my clients get into the "how" for achieving goals until they've told me their reasons why in a way that gives me goosebumps. (I always know if someone is talking from their heart about what they really want because I get goosebumps.) Do your life goals pass the Goosebumps Test? Is your desire big enough that it lights you up from the inside out? Does it make your heart sing? Does it just feel so "right?"

After you come up with your vision/desire/goals, determining your level of passion through your "whys" is the next step. Why do you want to achieve this particular thing? Let me assure you one heart-felt reason is worth 20 intellectual reasons. If reading the list of reasons why my clients want to achieve a particular goal puts me to sleep or fails the Goosebumps Test, then I get them to dig deeper and come up with more meaningful reasons why. If they can't do it, I suggest they consider changing their goals altogether because the goals they think they want might not really be theirs at all.

Other people's stuff

A lot of people I've worked with over the years—and myself at times—are carrying around someone else's list of the things they want to achieve in life. It might be a mother or father, sibling or uncle, teacher or religious leader filled with well-meaning intentions and lots of ideas about what success or a well-lived life is for them ... and they end up imposing their ideas on you and you don't even realize it. That's especially true if the person (or persons) involved are people you want to please or impress.

There's nothing wrong with getting great suggestions from other people. Maybe they help us get started in life. But somewhere along the line, if you truly want to be happy, fulfilled and authentically successful, you need to bring your own heart's desire to the table of life.

I believe the purpose of our lives is to fully express our authentic self in a way that serves our own evolution and that of other people if possible. We all have unique abilities, talents and desires inside us—a light burning inside—that we're here to express. It's important to listen to others. But at a certain point we have to start listening to that wise voice inside telling us to move in a particular direction, or work in a particular field, or start that business, or start that relationship, or start that family—whatever feels like our reason for being here.

Regardless of the external and measurable outcome, regardless of the opinions of others, it's important that we do what we came here to do. Sorry to go a little metaphysical on you, but life is not about observable success or failure as measured through society's filters. It's about feeling fully alive. And the way you do that is by being 100 percent authentically you, bringing your own unique gifts into the world.

So … what are your reasons for the big vision and desires in your life? If you haven't already really connected to your passions, if you haven't given them a bit of thought and airtime, I suggest you start getting comfortable with the idea. And if you're not sure right now, don't worry. It'll all come clearer as you move through the book and start putting those ticks in the boxes of Meaningful Goals, Daily Joy, Feeling Connected (with yourself) and Growing.

CHAPTER 6
Potential, Meaning and Choices

Potential

Here's an eye-opening exercise I do in my workshops and seminars. I ask everyone to raise their hand. Then I ask everyone in the room to leave their hand up if they believe they're using 100 percent of their full potential. Try it yourself. Raise your hand and leave it there if you're using *100 percent of your full potential.*

I've worked with CEO's, senior executives, entrepreneurs, successful business owners, multimillionaires, and elite athletes. To date I've yet to meet a single person who kept their hand in the air.

Regardless of how hard we're working or how fabulously we're showing up in life, we all have an innate sense that we're not tapping into our full potential. And when I ask people how much potential they think they're actualizing, even the greatest achievers say only about 50 percent. They know their potential is enormous. Which is why it's so great that you're expanding your horizons by reading this book.

I KNOW with *absolute certainty* we have not seen the best of you yet. I know that you're an untapped resource with enormous potential once you bring your best abilities into alignment, work on the areas that might be holding you back, and improve the areas in which you already excel.

I know you have an amazing amount of potential to make a huge difference in your life and the lives of others.

Meaning

A valuable Buddhist teaching is that all events are created ... neutral. Yep. In the Buddhist worldview nothing is good or bad. It only becomes so when we ascribe meaning to whatever's going on. Don't you know two people can see the same thing and one will think of it as "bad" and experience the emotions and reactions that go with "bad," while the other thinks of it as "good" and has a completely different emotional and physical response. It wasn't the event that caused the emotion. It was the *meaning* they gave it.

We tend to forget this while running on the hamster wheel of life. But it's a powerful piece of knowledge we can use to change our lives for the better. Remember in the last chapter we talked about our thoughts having a huge impact on the biochemistry and functionality of our bodies? That our thoughts create emotions that cause us to act in particular ways? And that both our thoughts and the consequent emotions affect us at a physical level, either hampering our bodies or helping heal them?

After all, the meaning we give something is really just a thought. And isn't it possible to change a thought? They aren't chiseled in stone and locked in a vault. We can change our thoughts in a heartbeat. Which means, if you can change a thought (including thoughts that carry a certain meaning), isn't it possible to deliberately create different emotional responses within your body just by changing your assessment (the meaning) of things?

The answer is yes, it's possible to change the meaning (a thought) we have about something and as a result change the impact on our bodies, our actions and our lives.

If you can see the logic of this and learn to master your thoughts and meaning-making, your life will never be the same again. If you can manage to see all events as neutral until you give them meaning ¬and deliberately choose the meaning you desire—you have the key to the kingdom of happiness.

For example, if you notice you're feeling bad about a situation, use self-awareness to observe the specific thoughts you have and the meaning of those thoughts and then change them. Ask yourself meaning-management questions like: "What is some good that exists in this situation? What might I have missed? What can I learn as a result of this situation? How can I grow from the lesson?"

Choice

Viktor Frankl wrote *Man's Search for Meaning* after having been a prisoner of war in a Nazi concentration camp in World War II. He suggested that even in the most appalling of situations, amidst constant fear of death, he still could choose the meaning to give to his experiences. He could choose the thoughts he would think and the emotions he would feed. The result? Frankl had a very different experience from others in the same situation.

Most of us find this a tough pill to swallow. But we *always* have a choice, even when we don't think we do. Some of our choices aren't easy. But if you look hard enough for a different angle with a fresh set of eyes and an open mind, there is *always* a choice.

We can choose to hang on to our anger, or we can choose to let it go. We can choose to stay in a destructive relationship or choose to experience the discomfort of leaving it. We can choose to stay in a job we hate or we can choose the uncertainty of leaving it. We can choose to have a tough conversation with a friend or partner, or we can choose to sweep issues under the carpet—or play the blame game.

A book I highly recommend on the subject of choice is *Choose The Life You Want*, written by Tal Ben-Sharar, PhD, a former professor at Harvard and a leader in Positive Psychology. Here are a few of my favorite chapter headings, to give you an idea about your ability to choose.

- Treat the work you do as a job OR experience your work as a calling
- Avoid learning from hardship OR actively learn the lessons of hardship
- Go through life as a fault-finder OR be a benefit-finder
- Refuse to accept reality OR accept reality and act on it
- Be part of the rat race OR focus on what truly matters

What choices are you making at the moment? Which choices are not serving you? Are you choosing to tell yourself you don't have a choice? Is there a different way you can look at something? Can you show up in a different way?

It's incredibly valuable to learn we always have a choice. Success is, in a large degree, about accepting responsibility for our internal and external states and choosing to make the best of them. So, next time you get stuck in what seems like a "bad" situation, ask yourself this question: "If there were a slim possibility there actually *is* another choice, what might it be?" Fire up that amazingly creative solution-finding brain of yours, and you'll be amazed how your life will change for the better.

CHAPTER 7

Power Versus Force

In 1994 Sir David R. Hawkins, MD, PhD, wrote an amazing book called *Power vs. Force*, revealing a method for accessing information about any thing or event, past or present, from what's termed the collective unconscious of humanity—even if you aren't a witness to that thing or event. He also made the distinction between the powerful flow of life force in nature, a power humans are subject to and yet can effortlessly direct to their advantage (if we're aware enough in consciousness to do so), versus having to use physical force combined with force of will to bludgeon our circumstances into order.

For example, when I'm using force, I'm working hard, exerting a lot of physical and mental effort to accomplish something—often against the flow of things. But when I'm tapped into this thing called "power," I'm able to align with the life energies and influence situations relatively effortlessly at an energetic level. I'm also tapping into the creative part of my brain (the frontal lobes of the cortex), coming up with ideas that are novel and unexpected that "grease the wheels" better than when I'm trying to accomplish something through force of logic and sheer determination alone.

On a practical level, when I'm trying to achieve something via force, I usually end up having to do ten steps to get to the final result. When I'm using power—meaning I'm in the flow of life and relaxed into an open, receptive creative consciousness—I can usually come up with an idea that bypasses a lot of steps, taking me much closer and much faster to the final result I want.

Whenever I realize I'm using too much force to make something happen (think trying to fit a square peg into a round hole), I take a step back, let go, and tap into my inner power of alignment with life and creativity to come up with an effective solution. Slowing down and relaxing or surrendering *into* a situation rather than working *at* something is basically the whole idea behind working smarter, not harder.

The physics of power vs. force

We can look at power and force in terms of quantum physics versus Newtonian physics. First let's talk about force. Force is relatable to Newtonian physics and the very clear laws and specific principles that apply to the physical world. If you hit a ball with a certain amount of force and you know the mass of the ball, you can calculate the acceleration of the ball with great mathematical accuracy and certainty. (Newton's Second Law of Motion: Force = mass x acceleration, or in this case it would be Acceleration = force/mass.)

However, the world starts getting weird when we get into quantum physics. In the realm of electrons, photons, muons and quarks, the rules of Newtonian physics don't apply. The quantum levels aren't physical. Instead, particles are understood to be made up of interpenetrating waves of energy/information. (In some theories energy and information are considered the same thing!)

Strangely, in the quantum world electrons can either "show up" as waves of energy or take on the properties of an actual particle. In something called the *double-slit experiment*, how the experiment is set up determines whether an electron shows up as a wave or as a particle. (If I'm confusing you (which is highly possible) I recommend you jump online and Google *double slit experiment* and learn how measurement aka "observation" affects electrons.) Even more strange, electrons can show up in multiple places at the same time (a phenomenon called superposition). And scientists can either know *where* an electron is or *how fast* it's traveling, but not both at the same time. Which is rather like clocking a baseball being thrown towards home plate at 102 miles an hour but not actually being able to locate the ball on the field!

I mention all this because when we start talking about power in terms of alignment with life energies and creativity you can see how subtle the dance between humans and the "physical" world really is.

Power, marketing specialists and talent shows

I often use this story to highlight the real-world application of power versus force when it comes to success.

Ever heard of Susan Boyle? She was the frumpy-looking, middle-aged woman from a small village in England who sang "I Dreamed a Dream" on the show *Britain's Got Talent* in 2009. (Her performance has been viewed on YouTube over 203 million times!) When Susan stepped on stage and declared she wanted to become a professional singer as famous of Elaine Paige, (a hugely popular professional English singer and actress) most people in the audience rolled their eyes.

Then she opened her mouth to sing. If you watch the video of her audition you will undoubtedly be emotionally moved. There is power at work and it's visible. She's not forcing anything. She's not trying to look like a babe or act like a star. She just taps into something bigger than herself, allows herself to become completely vulnerable and rocks it as her authentic self.

The audience went wild. The judges went wild. Within days her three-minute performance had gone viral online and she'd become an international sensation. Today she's a well-respected UK singer every bit as famous as Elaine Paige.

But what would have happened if frumpy (back then) Susan Boyle had walked into a high-end talent agency in London and told them she wanted to be as well-known as Elaine Paige? Most likely the executives would have said, "Are you insane? It will never happen," and sent her on her way. Or perhaps, if she had the money to pay for it, they would have humored her and drafted a Strategic Marketing Plan for her—a plan an inch thick outlining the 10 years and one hundred steps she needed to take to accomplish her goal.

This is a unique case of course, but I wanted to use it to highlight to you the significant gap between just trying to use mass-to-mass force and regular pathways to get what you want in life, versus tapping into the power of your life energy and creative brilliance.

Instead of waiting around and taking the long way, Susan tapped into the potential within her just waiting to get the chance to stand on center stage and let loose with all she had. Coming from the core of her being she utilized the unknown life intelligence that causes plants to grow, and seasons to change, and the animals to sense when an earthquake is about to erupt ... the unfathomable power that turns sperm and egg into a human being with a brain that has more synaptic connections than stars in the sky. I'm not saying that hard work and persistence aren't necessary. I'm just saying I'll be stuffed if I want to do it the hard way all the time.

I want to tap into the power and mystery that exists all around us. And

I want you to be open to the idea that success is not all about force, but rather the power within you that's just waiting to be expressed.

Practical use

I realize I don't know everything there is to know in the universe. I hardly know the tiniest fraction of a percent—and neither do people a lot smarter than me working in institutions with a lot more resources. I just approach the mystery in a practical fashion: 1) I work on getting clear what I want. 2) I come up with a well-thought-out, creative plan to achieve it and 3) apply appropriate strategies everyday. But I also realize much of what I want to make happen in my life can and will be taken care of by unknown forces beyond me. And I'm okay with that. In fact, I'm overjoyed. If I get where I want to get, all in one piece, and don't have to do all of the heavy lifting and figure it out the whole way, that's fine by me.

Where do awesome creative ideas come from? The ones that allow me to leapfrog past weeks or years of sweat and grind? I'm not 100 percent certain. But I'm sure as heck grateful!

I hope this helps you realize that while there are certain strategies that can take you to a whole new level of success, there might be more creative ways of achieving what you truly want. When you tap into more of your potential and more of your personal power it will surprise you by how high you can go in life and how wonderful the experience can be.

Just like Susan Boyle demonstrated so well, this principle is most at work when you're being your authentic self—when you're connected to yourself in a compassionate way; when you're feeling connected to something bigger than yourself; when you're moving in the direction of deeply meaningful goals; when you're allowing yourself to expand and grow, and when your health and vitality are augmenting the power source from within. All this is a part of being, experiencing and feeling authentic success.

CHAPTER 8
Your Personal Authentic Success Audit

I'd like you to take a quick subjective audit before you get started on the main material. That way you can identify the areas that might require more attention, and be more sensitive to tips, tools, and strategies that will benefit you most when you get to those sections.

Please get out your pen or pencil and take a few moments to complete this form before you read on.

Pillar	1 out of 10	10 out of 10	Rate
Daily Positive Emotions	Dread getting out of bed. Life sucks & everything in it. Angry & bitter. Lost. Untrusting. Uncertain.	Can't stop smiling. Bursting with gratitude & love for life. Sense of clarity and certainty.	8.5
High-quality Relationships	Disharmony. Stress. Toxicity. Resentfulness. Distrust. Anger. Frustration. Feeling unloved & disrespected.	So in love with the people in your life. Amazing intimate relationships. Feeling loved.	8

Pillar	1 out of 10	10 out of 10	Rate
Feeling Connected	Lonely. Disconnected. Feeling hollow inside. Life has no meaning. Fearful.	Deep sense of connection with God / Source / nature and the people on this Earth. Paradoxically you don't need props or people to feel deep connection to yourself and life.	8
Growing	Worse now than in the past. Going backwards – fast. Self-disappointment. Feel stagnant. Unfulfilled.	Always growing physically, mentally, emotionally and spiritually.	9
Meaningful Life Goals	Self centered. Narcissistic. All about instant gratification. Don't care about others or the planet.	Choosing & moving in the direction of goals that are deeply meaningful and will leave a positive legacy. Your goals align with your purpose & inspire passion.	9.5
Financial Flow	Constantly worried about money. Have none. In debt. Can't make any. Tight fisted with money.	Can create money anytime you want it. Never worry about money. More than enough. Give to others.	7+
Optimum Health & Vitality	Sick often. No energy. Chronic disease or illness. Always in pain.	Never get sick. High energy levels. Buzzing. Active. Strong. Resilient.	6
Aligned with Authentic Self	Feeling like a phony. Not doing work you like. Always influenced by others.	Living and working in a way completely aligned with your inner self. 100% authentic!	7.5+

PART 1:
MINDSET

CHAPTER 9
An Introduction to Mindset

Tony Robbins, one of the most sought-after success coaches in the world, says that success is *80 percent dependent on our personal psychology*. This is echoed by numerous teachers and relationship coaches and is easily observed by all of us when we look at the people we consider most successful. They just have a certain energy about them—a powerful vibe and an attitude of certainty.

When I ask people whether skills, opportunities, or attitude are most important for success, most come up with the same answer:

ATTITUDE!

We may wish that someone succeeds instead of us because they got lucky and had a great opportunity drop in their lap or because they have amazing skills that allowed them to succeed. But at a deeper level most of us know that the successful person has a superior attitude when it comes to success.

In the book *Grit: The Power of Passion and Perseverance*, Angela Duckworth, psychology professor at the University of Pennsylvania, presents compelling research that grit (strength of character, courage and resolve) is a greater predictor of success than IQ or talent.

Many children grow up with privilege, education, and crafted opportunities handed to them, only to crash and burn or achieve very little in the way of success and happiness. I'm sure you know people in your own life (or have observed them from afar) who've had amazing opportunities and yet their lives have been a total disaster.

So if skills aren't everything and opportunities don't guarantee success, then that leaves us with the biggest piece of the puzzle called attitude—that special way of psychologically showing up with passion, perseverance, and determination to get the success ball rolling.

In the *Oxford Dictionary Online* one definition of attitude is: "A settled way of thinking or feeling about something." And it's important to realize that thinking and feeling comes before behavior. The way we think determines how we feel. How we feel most often determines how we act and behave. And it's the collective experience of how we think, feel and behave that creates our attitude.

Once our thoughts, emotions and actions have settled into a repetitive pattern, it means our brains have developed fixed neurological networks— thought highways we cruise repeatedly. As a result, our attitudes are also locked into place. But that doesn't mean once our thoughts and attitudes have settled that that's it. Studies done by neuroscientists prove that our brains have the ability to transform neurologically over the course of our lives—an ability termed *neuroplasticity*. Our thoughts and attitudes are not fixed at all. They're just habits we can change. Which is really great to know.

If attitude is the external expression of our behavior and behavior is driven by our thinking and feeling and we want to cultivate an attitude that will lead us to success, then we obviously need to work on developing success-oriented thinking. This is what I call mindset. The right mindset is one of the key components to experiencing the internal and external expressions of authentic success.

Dr Joe Dispenza, an expert in neuroscience and brain plasticity, cites studies that show we're only conscious of our thinking and behavior about three to eight percent of the time. The remainder of the time we're running on subconscious programming flowing from a combination of our genetics and the environment we grew up in. But that's no excuse for staying stuck in old habits and mindsets anymore. Neuroplasticity of the brain reveals we can actually influence the physiology of the brain well into our senior—very senior—years. Powerful stuff indeed!

So, if we're almost always running on subconscious programming from our past, that means to get better results in life and make things happen in a manner more to our choosing, we need to work on two things:

1) We need to improve the quality of our conscious thinking by becoming more present and aware of our thoughts and

2) Learn to recognize when we're running on autopilot and revise our subconscious programming

In this section on mindset, we're going to start exploring what we can do, or stop doing, in order to optimize our mental faculties and align our mindset with goals that will better serve us as we move forward in life. We want to learn how to positively influence our psychology and behavior and create an attitude which allows us to have a positive impact on those around us and the world at large.

CHAPTER 10
Beliefs & Stories

Our beliefs control our lives, and the vast majority of our beliefs are not actual facts. I may believe something and be 100 percent convinced it's a fact. But that doesn't make it so. All it takes is one person proving the opposite is true and my "fact" crumbles to fiction. And yet even if it's not true, my belief remains a self-fulfilling prophecy. Why do I say that? Because beliefs impact our mental and emotional state and our mental and emotional states affect our behavior and our behavior determines the results we reap in life.

I tell all my coaching clients, "I don't give a damn what your beliefs are. I only care about how they make you *feel*." If you believe, "When I cross my fingers on my right hand, while balancing on my left foot and closing my right eye, it makes me more creative," guess what? It actually makes you feel empowered and creative. Which is what I care about. Therefore I'm totally supportive of your quirkiness.

Truly, it's not so much what your beliefs are, it's about how they make you FEEL. If you feel more empowered standing on one foot with your fingers crossed, you're in an elevated emotional state that is more conducive to creativity: alert, energized, calm, focused, and in the present moment.

This doesn't mean I don't challenge a lot of my clients' stories and beliefs. I do. And it pisses some of them off that I spend a good deal of my time (and theirs) doing it until they finally realize that I never challenge the stories that make them feel good. I challenge the ones that make them feel bad. And it's easy to see which beliefs are empowering and which ones aren't. Their body language and pitch, pace and tone of their voices change when their beliefs constrict and limit them or cause them to go into a fear response.

Bottom line the stories we tell (as opposed to the facts) have a huge impact on the results we get in life. Which is why I coach people on learning how to tell when they're in the midst of some belief/story that's limiting their lives. To do that I coach them to 1) slow down, 2) get present, 3) get conscious of what they're saying, and then 4) challenge the stories and statements they're making that make them feel disempowered.

When we discover the stories/beliefs that are holding us back (whether fact or fiction, it doesn't matter), then we have the choice to be greater than the story. Here's a common example of the kind of stories I'm talking about—and this story is only one word long: *can't*.

What a show-stopper! Most people have a lot of stories in their heads about what they can't do. "Skydive? Charge $500 an hour? Lose 100 pounds? *I can't!*"

My best advice is to remove the word CAN'T from your vocabulary. Replace it with phrases like, "I haven't figured it out yet," or "I'm still working on it," or "Let me do some research," or "Let me think or meditate or talk to someone about it." BAM!!! You're still in the game! You're creating the opportunity to let a whole new story that empowers you and allows all sorts of possibilities to unfold.

Speaking of stories…

I remember working with a client in Rome. The first time I saw her she entertained me in her swanky city apartment where she proceeded to tell me this sob story about how she was done wrong by her ex-husband and how it continued to influence her life and how all these bad things were happening as a result. The second time I saw her she started recounting the same story. I stopped her and said, "Listen, this story you're holding onto isn't entertaining. In fact, it's really bringing down my energy and yours. Plus, I've already heard it once. And that was more than enough."

I pointed out that every time she told the story, she was literally conjuring up and reliving the miseries of the past. "The brain can't tell the difference between something real and something remembered," I said. "Every time you tell this story your brain releases the same chemicals that made you feel terrible back when it was happening and it forces you to have the same experience over and over."

I pointed out that when we tell a story from the past we're effectively living in the past—that telling such stories makes us less resourceful dealing with our current situation. It saps our life force and holds us back from the very real possibility of creating a much more inspiring future. And I coached her to tell a new story.

Neuro-Linguistic Programming

According to the system of Neuro-Linguistic Programming (NLP), there are three major components involved in creating human experience: neurology, language and programming. The brain system (neurology) regulates our body's functions, language determines how we connect with others in the world, and our programming determines the kinds of pictures and stories of the world we create. The people who are most effective in the world are those who have a story (or "map" in NLP lingo) of the world that allows them to perceive the greatest number of available choices and perspectives.

In the NLP school of thought, "The past does not equal the future" because we are capable of reframing past events and looking at them from a new point of view any time we choose. This reframing—this conscious shifting of perspective—changes our thoughts and thus our brain chemistry, our emotions, and thus our future actions and decisions … and thus our future.

It's always possible for us to pave a completely new path. Just because we've made bad choices in the past doesn't mean we must continue to be defined by those choices. I can be arrested and end up in court and in that moment in the courtroom decide to "show up" differently. Even if I'm convicted and sent to prison, I can choose to show up differently. Instead of continuing to define myself as a "criminal" or a "vengeful dude," I can decide to educate myself in prison. I can choose to write a book. I can choose to lead an entire country into reform, like a certain amazing man by the name of Nelson Mandela.

Be the author of your own stories. What do you want the story to be? Who do you want to be? How do you want to show up? What do you want to have in your life?

Where attention goes, energy flows.

Who is in control of the direction of your attention? You. Me. All of us. That's the one thing we definitely have control of. Maybe we don't have control over the thousands of thoughts that pop into our heads each day. But we can CHOOSE what to focus on and thus give our energy. And the more focus and energy we give something the grander the result.

What stories are you telling yourself?

Are you telling yourself you can or you can't? Are you telling yourself that you'll never get what you want? Are you telling yourself that you don't deserve all the good things waiting for you? Are you telling yourself that relationships are hard or that you might get hurt? That it's safer to avoid intimacy and depth in your relationships? Are you telling yourself you'll never earn over $100,000 a year because _____ (fill in the blank)? Are you telling yourself as a woman over 35 in Hollywood you'll never pick up any meaningful work?

At the time of writing this chapter, I'd just come back from attending a training course in Los Angeles. While I was there I met a client in the entertainment industry who actually did tell me a story about how she refused to tell people her age because she felt it affected her acting prospects. Guess what I said?

I suggested she stop buying into the story and create a new story instead—a story that was near and dear to her heart—a story that was not so dependent on the shallow opinions of others. Right then and there she told me she'd already created a character – Lady Love - and wanted to do her own comedy show as this character. As she talked about Lady Love—an awesome, edgy character that played with relationship and love issues and shook audiences up—she got excited. She chucked her depleting story about being too old to work in Tinsel Town into the rubbish bin where it belonged. And right before my eyes she lit up— totally transformed and enlivened as she talked about changing the lives and relationships of her future audiences.

So here's the chapter takeaway:
1. People are AWESOME. *You* are awesome.
2. We have power and potential within us that is *enormous*.

3. We limit ourselves with the stories we have about work, relationships, money, success, health, etc.—stories we tell and beliefs we buy into that play on an endless loop in our minds, sucking us dry.
4. Our stories/beliefs affect brain chemistry and emotions and determine our choices and thus our future.
5. Change your story and you change your life.

Practice

Here's a simple way to discover some of the disempowering beliefs you're lugging around in your head. Take a few moments to complete the following sentences. And remember: awareness is the first step to transformation.

1. I believe intimate relationships are_____.
2. I believe money is _____.
3. I believe I am_____.
4. The area in my life where I experience the most pain, challenge or discomfort is_____.
5. A story I'm telling myself that causes pain or discomfort is_____.

Also, here's a little exercise from author/teacher Byron Katie—a master at busting apart disempowering stories with a process she calls The Work. (She's also the author of the book *Loving What Is*. One of my favorite quotes is, "When I argue with reality I lose. But only 100 percent of the time.") Ha!

So, pick one of your favorite disempowering statements and ask yourself Katie's four questions below:

1. Is the statement true?
2. Can you be absolutely 100 percent sure the statement is true?
3. How does having this statement make you feel?

4. How would you feel without this statement?

Can you see how a statement might just be a story or belief as opposed to something that is 100 percent reality? Getting a handle on our beliefs and stories is life-changing work and definitely essential when it comes to authentic success.

PS – I've written a mini-book on beliefs and how they control our lives, which you can download off my website **www.carlmassy.com** to go even deeper.

CHAPTER 11
On Identity

I heard Tony Robbins say the following during a seminar and it's stuck with me: "People have a strong need to stay consistent with their identity." Add to that the fact that our brains lock in repetitive thought patterns by creating densely connected neuron firing patterns that get more deeply grooved and habitual as time goes on—and all too frequently we end up operating on automatic, playing out roles, spouting stories, and having emotional reactions … all without a moment's thought or hesitation.

Back in the day the classical Greek philosopher Socrates recommended getting to "know thyself." He even went so far as to proclaim "the unexamined life isn't worth living."

There's no more fundamental question in life than, "Who am I?" What does it mean to "have" an identity? Ever wondered where the heck your identity—your sense of self—comes from? Well, just in case you haven't asked the question before, let's have a wee look under the covers of who you are right now.

Looked at strictly from the physical perspective, it could be said that each one of us is the sum of our genetic programming (which you will learn is a lot less impactful then you imagine), plus mental, emotional, and behavioral conditioning. I'm not going to get into a debate over the percentages of nature versus nurture here. Let's just agree we're influenced by both our million-year-old genetic code passed down to us from our ancestors, plus all the life experiences we've had from the point of conception onwards.

(For those of you who would like to go further down the rabbit hole and include the influence of the soul or a higher consciousness or collective consciousness or the unified quantum field, we're going to shelve that for a bit. *The Guidebook to This Thing Called Spirituality* is the 5th book planned in my series, but it's still a couple years away. For the moment (as you will soon see), it's enough to deal with our physical coding and programming.)

Bottom line, if we're ever going to "know ourselves," we've got to get a handle on how amazingly programmed and conditioned we are. Not until we recognize our programming and break past what we believe we *ought* to see and think and believe can we perceive the world more accurately.

The following exercise from Tony Robbins is a great de-cloaking tool. I've seen enormous shifts happen with my clients when they do this exercise because when you have an "ah-hah moment" (an internal shift), *your external reality shifts.*

So find that pen and paper again and get started.

Question 1
Whose love, attention and affection did you crave the most when you were growing up? dad + mom

(For me it was my father. I knew my mum loved me pretty much unconditionally, so I did not feel that I had to work as hard to get my mother's love. So my focus was on getting the love of my father. For you it might be a father, a mother, an older sibling, a grandparent, another family member, teacher or other social role model.)

Question 2
Who did you have to be in order to get that love? What did you have to be like? felt like I couldnt make mistakes.

(I believed I had to be hard-working, high performer who never made mistakes, well-behaved, neat and tidy, organized, in control, obedient, honest, respectful, a stand out, courageous, non-disruptive, and adventurous. Whew! Sure, a lot of these qualities have been incredibly beneficial. But others were just as well left in the past.)

Question 3
Who weren't you allowed to be if you wanted to get that love?
myself

(I wasn't permitted to be loud, disruptive, out of control, indecisive, reckless, crazy, spontaneous, unorganized, impulsive, disrespectful or rude. Winging it and taking risks were out of the question as well.)

Question 4
Who do you like, admire and respect a lot and what is it about them that you like?

(I dig people like Einstein, who was a super-smart, deep thinker but quirky and authentic, plus the Dalai Lama who is powerful, authentic, fun, spiritual and compassionate.)

Questions 5
Who do you dislike a lot and what is it about them that you dislike?

(I really dislike intimidating, totally arrogant, annoying braggarts who love telling other people how great they are.)

How to use your responses
I strongly encourage you to do this exercise right now before you read on. Yes, it seems simple and maybe even obvious. But don't be fooled. More than one client has done this and "Holy s---!" was only one of many things they said in surprise.

Basically it's designed to tell you why you act the way that you do. You may not still be striving to win that person's love. But you'll discover your actions are still being habitually influenced by them—which is great in some cases, but not in others.

You'll also understand who you are NOT allowed to be. Which can be problematic because in many cases this may be EXACTLY who you need to be to achieve the goals you want to achieve. For instance, if I want to succeed as an entrepreneur, do you think it would be handy for me to be a risk taker, impulsive, willing to interrupt people (as I pitch my ideas or products), and sometimes get started without a 100 percent complete plan? You bet! That's exactly what I need to be. But to be that I had to become aware of the decades of unconscious conditioning preventing me from being able to express these behaviors.

Question four gives a better idea of what you can aspire to be. Having positive role models is great for accountability in being all we can be.

And finally we come to question five, which is not the most fun place to hang out. But have you ever heard the theory that everyone is a mirror for us to learn from? That quite often things that frustrate us about other people are the things that frustrate us about ourselves? Or perhaps the people who piss us off do so because they're free to express themselves in ways our programming won't allow?

I remember a public speaker I saw that I *totally* disliked within about 43 seconds. He SO rubbed me up the wrong way I'm actually tempted to name him here and now so you'll never to see this guy. (That would be going a bit far, I know—although he'd probably lap up the free publicity.) Anyway, when I considered if there where things I disliked in him that I actually needed to evoke in myself, I realized much of my frustration was about me, not him.

Although I'd never present myself in such an inauthentic way, he made me realize a frustration I have about myself. Namely, I don't self-promote enough to attain the level of professional success I desire and positively influence the greatest number of people. Bottom line, he was obnoxious, sure. But a lot of the triggering was about showing me I had something to work on. Doing this exercise made me realize where I needed to step up my game.

Here's another example of this mirroring dynamic. Perhaps you're a well-organised and structured person and a bit on the controlling side. You might be totally triggered by someone at work who is casual, relaxed and spontaneous. You look at them and bitch about how that person doesn't care, or doesn't pull their weight or is a disruptive influence because that's the way you see them. Yet at a deeper level maybe you envy their ability to be carefree because you realise your "over-caring" actually causes you (and others) huge amounts of stress.

So, again, I strongly encourage you to do this activity as soon as possible.

And if you're having a challenge trying to interpret what's coming up for you, then drop me a line and I'll see what we can uncover together.

One last thing ... before I go to the next chapter I want you to ponder this idea: *What got you to the level of success you're experiencing today, is the same thing that's holding you back from going to the next level.*

Maybe that rock-solid, highly-structured plan in the past got you to a reasonable level of success. But now the thing that will take you to a much higher level is being more creative, intuitive, daring, unstructured, and unplanned.

What has got you to your current level of success?

How might this be holding you back?

And what might be another thing you need to do?

CHAPTER 12

Thinking Patterns

A lot of people think they think a lot. But what they're actually doing is entertaining a bunch of repetitive thoughts. And there's not only a HUGE difference in the act, there's a HUGE difference in the results as well.

The difference between real thinking and what I call "thoughting" is that the first is highly present and original and the other is based in past experiences and results. Thinking is highly conscious and creative and "thoughting" is rote and almost completely unconscious. Thinking is about utilizing the amazing creative power of your mind—a mind that is without limits. Thinking is about creating and manifesting entirely new possibilities and results. It's purposeful and constructive. You're figuring something out, or planning something, or trying to logic something through in your life. "Thoughting" is mental masturbation .

When you're really thinking, you CHOOSE what images to play in your mind and you direct your internal dialogue. Thinking is exciting. You end up feeling the way you want to feel—enthusiastic, inspired, maybe even a little scared if you're dreaming big.

"Thoughting" is a lot of uncontrolled automatic rehashed blah blah in the brain: "Did I pay the VISA bill? Why did Fred get that promotion? What's wrong with me? I'll never get ahead. I can't believe he stuck me with the lunch tab the other day. Cheap bastard. My VISA bill is out of control. I'll never get ahead. Did I pay the VISA bill?"

Thoughting is non-constructive and steers us in circles. Thoughting makes us depressed. You're thousands of times more likely to achieve what you want in life if you're purposeful in your thinking and cut way back on the *thoughting* thing—which is guaranteed to give you the same results and the same old life you're already leading.

One thing that can help you make the switch from repetitive past to exhilarating present—from thoughting to thinking—is by doing a hack on your emotions.

You can choose to feel a particular emotion, for example, joy, without a triggger thought to make you feel joyful. The way to do this hack is to *change your physiology*. If I want to feel immediate joy, I move my facial muscles into a smile. This change in my physiology triggers an automatic emotional response and my whole being lightens up—which then makes it easier to think thoughts related to joy instead of repetitive thoughts about whether I can pay my VISA bill. Truly, changing your physical state changes your emotions. It's one of the reasons I love to dance in my office. Pure joy!

The right mindset

One of my favorite books is *Mindset*, written by Dr Carol Dweck, a psychology professor with a specialty in motivation, personality and development. She came up with a theory about intelligence that examines two predominant types of mindset that are eerily close to thoughting and thinking: a fixed mindset and a growth mindset.

Generally, someone with a fixed mindset believes certain things—they're either good at something or not. They're either smart or dumb, a good dancer or a bad dancer, a creative person or not creative, etc. etc. and nothing can be done about it. They're stuck. They unconsciously believe they "are the way they are"—limited by their genes, biology, physiology, education, etc. And it's all based in past experiences. If they've failed at something once, they unconsciously believe they'll always fail.

Dweck also discovered that people who tend towards a fixed mindset also tend to decide if they're good at something (or not) after only a short time of trying something new. If they experience immediate failure, instead of persisting, they decide "I'm just not the right type of person to waterski" and will quickly give it up.

On the other hand a person with a growth mindset unconsciously believes they'll get better at whatever it is they try. They know if they learn as much as they can, practice, test and adjust their methodology, do the mental and/or physical work—maybe even hire a coach—they'll inevitably get better at the task. And it doesn't matter what it is: Learning a new language, writing a noteworthy book, learning a new sport, becoming better in social engagements, learning to publicly speak, or any other new skill. They have a "can do" attitude versus a "can't do" attitude.

But remember: Attitudes and thoughts are not chiseled in stone. As I've pointed out, the latest research in neuroscience has proven that the brain is not hard-wired. Instead of neurons dying off as we get older (as was once supposed), we now know that the brain creates new neurons throughout life—a process called neurogenesis.

The point I REALLY want you to get is this: **You can get better at anything you put your mind to**. Change and growth are part of life. It just requires focused mental attention and a desire to do so. It requires learning, testing and adjusting. Sometimes it means getting a specialist to help show you the way. Basically your brain is like putty in your hands. It's magical and powerful. But ... you need to use it. You need to learn to consciously and purposefully think instead of being a slave to repetitive thoughts based in the past.

And one of first things you need to do to get on this growth path is realize how easily thoughts become habitual.

We all have physical behavioral habits, like automatically sucking in our stomach when we see someone attractive, or chewing our lip or twirling our hair. It helps to understand we have thinking habits as well—patterns of thought which are helping us or potentially harming us. Our aim is to develop thinking habits that are highly beneficial to how we feel and act, thus creating positive results in life.

Here's an example of an ineffective thoughting pattern:
1. A negative thought pops into your head: *I'm just no good at job interviews.*
2. You become fixated on it.
3. It makes you feel bad.
4. You start imagining (in hi-def surround-sound) how this "fact" is going to screw things up for you in your next interview.
5. You exaggerate the potential consequences: *If I don't get this job I'll be a joke in this town.*
6. Now you feel absolutely terrible and terrified. Plus you've activated the fight or flight nervous system response in the body, which is amplifying the negative feelings you're experiencing.

On the other hand if you use **conscious thinking**:
1. You monitor your thoughts.
2. You recognize the fixed negative thought: *I'm just no good at job interviews.*
3. You choose what you want. I want to have a good job interview.

4. Instead of imaging a terrible interview you create an image in your mind of what you want.
5. You increase the brightness of the picture and add some additional sensory inputs like sound and texture.
6. You play an internal dialogue, which supports the image.
7. You choose what you would like to feel.
8. You start moving and feeling the way you want to feel.

All of this starts you priming the brain up for the thing you want. Your reticular activating system (RAS) starts getting clear about what you want. You see the image. You hear the internal dialogue that supports what you want. And you feel the feelings you'd feel if you'd already achieved the thing you want: Acing the interview.

Then you take action. You think about all the major points you want to make during the interview. You write them down. You role play with a friend until you feel comfortable. Then you go do the interview.

This is the way to do the thinking/creating thing. But like the integration of any habit, you need to practice it. You need to make time for it. You need to consciously do it—time and time again. You need to learn to catch yourself when you're on a hamster wheel thinking negatively and unconstructively. Then follow through with the steps above. Eventually you'll get there and you'll have a new and highly beneficial thinking pattern going for you!

Remember: You can be the master of your mind *if* you take the time to do the work. I know you have it in you. And now that you know you have a flexible brain and the ability to create a whole new mindset, you're well on your way to mastering your mind and creating the success in life you're worthy of.

CHAPTER 13
Consciousness

Consciousness is a super big, super intangible subject that appears to be at the opposite end of the spectrum of everything that's finite. And yet there are some people, like philosopher David Chalmers, who believe that everything we perceive as finite is actually made from consciousness. Needless to say, scientists and philosophers and psychologists haven't figured it out yet. Perhaps they never will.

But that doesn't mean we shouldn't try.

Many years ago I ran across a very cool definition of a warrior: "A warrior is a person who desires the answers to the bigger questions about life and is ready to journey into the unknown to uncover the answers. A warrior knows s/he may never find the answers. But they go into the unknown regardless."

We may never find THE answer, but right now I want you to be a warrior and as open-minded as possible as we step into the unknown realm called "consciousness." And yes, it really does have something to do with authentic success.

More than just mental

I don't have understand exactly how energy in the form of electricity works in order to turn the lights on or charge my smartphone. I simply flick the light switch and plug the phone in. The same is true of consciousness. I may not fully understand where it comes from (though I have my own opinions ;-), but I can still use it to the fullness of its potential.

Consciousness, as it applies to human beings, is our overall state of awareness. This includes mental acuteness, but also something a lot more subtle—what I call intuition. The higher my state of overall mental and intuitive awareness, the more optimally I function, the better choices I make, the better results I'm likely to get. Makes sense. Right? Just as poor choices lead to bad results and a bucket load of tears or worse.

Most setbacks in my early life—like getting arrested for disorderly conduct when I was an on-call Duty Officer for my army unit, or ending up in the hospital after somersaulting off the counter in a bar (onto a concrete floor) to impress a very attractive woman, or crashing my car doing post-party donuts in a field, or ... well, you get the picture— all these things resulted from very poor choices made while under the influence of excessive amounts of Bundaberg Rum and Coca-Cola—a condition I now understand was a lowered state of consciousness. (Being unaware that somersaulting from a height onto concrete while drunk might not have happy consequences is definitely an experience of lower consciousness!)

What I now know is that *the higher the level of my consciousness*, the better decisions I am likely to make and therefore the greater the results I am likely to achieve. So, if you want to succeed at a whole new level, you need to dedicate yourself to the understanding and application of raising consciousness.

The reality about consciousness

How many times have you heard somebody say in the midst of some life drama, "I don't know how this happened to me?" (Or said it yourself.) As I've pointed out, most human beings are only consciously aware of what they're doing and thinking about three to eight percent of the time. The other 92 to 97 percent of the time we're running on subconscious programs—what I call autopilot. This means we're mostly unaware (unconscious) of the thoughts we have and thus the feelings we generate, the behaviours we perform and the results we get.

We don't have to be conscious of everything. We can't be. The brain handles billions of functions every second at the cellular level in our bodies without our ever knowing about it. And that's a good thing. What's not a good thing is having limiting, disempowering thoughts, and beliefs that are just plain wrong, running on autopilot.

Our target goal is to increase the *frequency* and *potency* of the consciousness we bring to the most important decisions in our lives as well as to the day-to-day stuff. Little details and small choices—finishing work we start, listening to people around us, paying attention to what's needed in any given situation, making the right food choices for our health—add up.

The good news is we can increase our level of consciousness by doing specific practical activities. We may not understand the exact interplay between our mind/consciousness and our physical brains (the puzzling interaction scientists refer to as "the hard problem of consciousness"), but we don't have to. I know with a high level of certainty that by doing certain things in certain ways we can change the level of consciousness we bring to our lives and therefore change the results we experience.

Whether that's enhanced relationships, more joy doing what you love, or more financial flow, increasing your consciousness is the pathway to leveling up. In fact, it's one of my overarching intentions to constantly raise my level of consciousness over the course of my life. This goal serves as a constant guide, helping me make practical decisions big and small. I'm always asking myself, "Will this choice in front of me raise or lower my conscious awareness? Will it distract me? Hinder me? Make me a smaller person?"

This is the kind of conscious thinking we have to do to get to the future we desire.

Practical techniques for increasing consciousness

I encourage you at some stage to take a deeper dive into the topic of consciousness by reading *The Guidebook to Optimum Health*, where I go into a lot more detail. For our current purposes, I will simply hit on a few key points.

The holiest, most practiced, most practical activity for increasing our level of conscious awareness is *meditation*. Thousands of years of practice by countless men and women and at least four decades of scientific research prove this is so.

Meditation increases my *creativity* so I come up with better ideas and solutions. It increases my *equanimity* so I can calmly make better decisions and access my brain's superpowers without getting emotionally blown off course over stuff. It increases my ability to *focus* so I can concentrate better on the details when I need to. It increases my *perspective* so I can see the whole picture. It increases my *awareness* through my senses, intuition and my kinesthetic (feeling) body. It relaxes me. Meditation and other mindfulness activities are superfood for the brain and bolster every aspect of consciousness that can help us live successful lives.

If formal meditation seems too far out, you can still increase your level and capabilities of consciousness by increasing the depth and consistent regulation of your breathing. One of the key elements to meditation is active and conscious breathing. By increasing the depth and quality of your breathing you increase the amount of oxygen you feed all the cells in your body—including the brain.

An energized, oxygen-enriched brain can actively facilitate a state of increased consciousness. A brain fried from too much computer work and/or *thoughting*, a brain depleted in oxygen and available energy through a lack of exercise and poor food choices is a numb brain, always on the verge of going to sleep. It's certainly not the brain you want to take to a business meeting or on a first date!

The food and water thing

Ever heard the phrase "You are what you eat?" Well, I want to play with that statement a little bit and suggest that how good or bad you feel, think and act is based on what you eat and drink—or on what you don't eat and drink. In fact, I want to do more than suggest it. I will state it pure and simple: The food and drink you ingest are the key sources for energy in your body—the energy your body needs to digest, eliminate, detoxify and repair the body, plus a bazillion other things.

Now, if a large part of the energy we ingest is used to metabolize and eliminate crappy processed foods and sugary drinks, the end result is less energy (life force) available to fully express our awesomeness. If you eat highly processed foods with numerous additives (and really hard to pronounce names) you can be sure that you're hindering, rather than helping, optimum functioning in your life.

The brain comprises only about three percent of our body weight, but it consumes over 20 percent of the available energy in our bodies. When it comes to consciousness, a poor supply of fuel directly affects the amount of energy available for brain function. We need a well-fuelled brain to access our full mental faculties and tap into higher states of consciousness.

All energy (in the form of calories) is not the same. In the 7,000-year-old yogic tradition it's understood that different foods have different levels of vitality or energy (called prana or life force). Based on thousands of years of experimentation, yogi's and Buddhist monks have come to advocate a plant-based diet as a way for them to tap into higher levels of consciousness.

 I can definitely feel a different level and kind of vitality if I eat an apple versus a sugar-laden chocolate bar. When I remove processed foods and consume less sugar (which is mood altering), when I ingest fewer synthetic chemicals (who knows what they're doing to us), and eat less stuff that's been sitting on a shelf for months at a time, I feel better. A LOT better. I'm more conscious when I follow a predominantly whole-food plant-based diet because there's life left in live foods (aka: fruit and vegetables). When we eat more of them, we experience their vitality and radiant energy (measured in hertz and not kilojoules). But don't take my word for it. I encourage you to experiment for yourself.

The rest thing

When you're tired you don't function well. The body goes into more of a survival mode and you don't have access to your higher faculties. Awareness/consciousness dulls. Although science cannot say definitively why we need to sleep or what sleep exactly does for our brains and bodies, it's obvious to any of us that we perform a lot better when we're rested. My advice? Stop watching TV until late, or surfing the Internet, or vegging out gaming and get to bed! Most people need at least 7.5 hours sleep a night. You might think you can thrive on less, but most likely you're just surviving. So get enough sleep and stop missing out on a higher level of potentiality.

More on Emotions

The neo-cortex (the upper part of the brain) is where higher mental processes like creativity, innovation, and willpower take place. Neuroscientists have discovered that the middle part of the brain—the limbic brain—is the seat of emotional processing. This is where the infamous amygdala and hypothalamus hang out, two major players in the activation of the stress response. Emotions are handled in a totally different place away from the more evolved and more creative pre-frontal lobes, connected to consciousness.

If we don't understand how to process our emotions, in particular the ones that relate to a stress response, it's very hard to regulate consciousness. Ever had your mind hijacked by an emotional storm? Who hasn't? Thing is, if we're using the middle part of the brain (also called the mammalian brain) we have the mental faculties of a mammal. In other words, when I go into a reactive emotional state, I have the brainpower of my dog. Sure, my dog is cute and all that. But she's definitely not able to process much beyond her next meal, her walk and how to get more petting.

We all need to learn how to handle our emotions better. One of the best ways is through—yep, you guessed it—meditation. Through meditation we calm the brain, in particular the mammalian part of the brain, so we can become more conscious of what's happening internally and externally around us.

Other emotional management techniques that I've found effective are: Emotional Freedom Technique (check out *The Tapping Solution* by Nick Ortner), the See Feel Hear Technique (check out *The Heart of the Matter* by Dr Darren Wiessman and Cate Montana), Neuro Linguistic Programming (NLP), guided meditation recordings (check out Dr Joe Dispenza), hypnotherapy, journaling, and various other mindfulness techniques. It's well worth exploring different techniques to find ways to self-manage and fully express your emotions in a way that is life enhancing.

Willpower

What is willpower? Mr Google defines it as: *Control deliberately exerted to do something or to restrain one's own impulses.* If you break the word in two it becomes the power to exert our will. What, then, is my will? Is it consciously determined or biologically determined or socially programmed? And down the rabbit hole we go.

Willpower drives our ability to get done what we deem most important for us. Willpower can be active, as in the drive to do something. Or it may be about refraining from doing something active. Either way willpower is our regulator. But willpower doesn't just happen. It's very much dependent upon having a clear idea of what you want to achieve—which is why having a clear vision is so important.

I can have great willpower. But if I have a crap vision and plan, I'll end up where I don't want to be. Which is pretty much the opposite of success.

The part of the brain most related to willpower is the pre-frontal lobe. This is the part of the brain that says "Yes" to action or "No" to a really stupid idea. Research indicates this part of our brain goes through several growth spurts before it's fully developed. The first spurt is up to about seven years of age, and the second is from around puberty until somewhere in our 20's.

Car insurers have been aware of this for decades. It's why young people (especially guys) have to pay such high-premium rates. The companies realize the likelihood of someone making dumb decisions before age 25 is pretty high. (Drag race anyone?)

Lack of willpower may be related to brain development as well as a number of physiological factors. As I said, when we fire up the neo-cortex it consumes high amounts of energy. Which means we don't want to be willy-nilly in our use of willpower. Overuse can exhaust the brain just like overuse can tax our muscles.

Just as a muscle needs the right fuel to operate optimally, it needs to be well hydrated, it needs adequate rest, it needs the right level of resistance (enough, but not too much), and it needs to be trained on a regular basis. The same thing for the brain.

So don't sign up for things that require maximum use of your brain when you're tired, hungry, and dehydrated. Don't have tough conversations with your partner immediately after one of you gets back from a grueling day at work.

Give yourselves some down time. Relax. Eat. Drink water. Get out for a walk in nature before you start yapping. If you don't you'll be more reactive (coming from the emotional midbrain), you'll be less creative, and you'll be more likely to say things you'll later regret.

Can you relate to any of this? Likewise at work don't plan meetings for times when people are likely to be hungry, dehydrated and tired. Plan for your most creative work to take place in the mornings or after quality breaks.

IF-THEN Strategy

If you've read my other books, you've likely heard this before, but it's a great strategy. Just yesterday I was using it with a client to great effect. The If-Then strategy relates to priming, which I've spoken about already. (Remember the Will Smith movie called *Focus* where they primed somebody's mind to make a choice they thought was their own, but actually it was strategically implanted?) Or maybe you've heard the term "contingency planning"?

The strategy is simple: Before you implement an idea you consider the potential obstacles along the way and develop contingency plans. And you do this when you're fresh and not under pressure. That way instead of flapping around like a headless chicken trying to figure out what to do if your plan goes south, you just open up the contingency plan and following the steps.

The If-Then strategy works by priming your brain to automatically switch into a contingency plan rather than needing to fire up your frontal cortex to figure out something out on the spot and then implement it. That's hard work and rarely ends up with positive results.

Here's an example: Decide ahead of time before you go to a party, "IF

I get offered an alcoholic drink THEN I will say, "No, thank you" and reach for a glass of soda. That way instead of getting to the party and getting carried away with the energy and high times and saying "Oh, what the hell. Maybe I'll just have one," you've primed your brain to succeed with your decision to not drink.

Another example might be: IF I haven't eaten anything in the last couple hours THEN I will not go shopping at the convenience store (which is packed with sugary temptations).

Can you see how effective this is? It's about utilizing your mind most effectively to make the best decisions while you're most conscious.

Staying present

Last but far from least, it's vital that we be awake and aware in *the present moment*—a place called *the eternal now*.

It's actually impossible to be anywhere but here and now. But so much of the time we end up being "present" to the past or the future. We're here now, but instead of our minds being alert and conscious of what's going on around us and within us, our heads are lost in some old story, or we're worried about some future event. A classic example is driving down the highway lost in thought, rehashing a business meeting that didn't go well (in the past), or worrying about how to pay for your 12-year-olds college tuition (in the future). Suddenly you "wake up" and get present and don't even know how you got to where you are!

So often our internal programs, beliefs and habitual stories (thoughting) lead us into a disempowered emotional state. Once an emotional program is in motion it's much harder to be the type of person you want to be or make the choices that will allow you to experience the highest levels of authentic success.

We also don't pay enough attention to what's going on inside. Ever have a gut feeling about something that you ignored and lived to regret that you didn't pay better attention? We all have. In our materialistic world, we've become fixated on the external environment as a means of feedback on what is right, wrong, good and bad. We listen to others. We get fooled by outside circumstances—temporary fame turns our head. We confuse money and big houses with success. As a result we don't learn how to tap into the internal environment and wisdom that resides within us.

Remember as we close this section that your internal psychology has a huge impact on your external results. Through being aware, you can actually change your internal state, programs and ultimately your external behavior. You are extremely powerful. So develop a mindset that is empowered. Develop a mindset that is self-aware. Develop a mindset that is flexible to change. Develop a mindset that is open to new ideas and information. Develop a mindset where your conscious mind is firmly in control, not your body, random thoughts or reactive emotions.

I know you've got this! Good for you. NOW Do it!

PART 2:
STRATEGIES

CHAPTER 14
An Introduction to Strategies

As an officer in the Australian Army for 14 years (it's hard to imagine I was once Major Massy!), and a consultant to numerous Olympic Games and Asian Games, I learned to be quite the strategist. But what do I mean by that?

In the most simplistic sense, being strategic means thinking and planning before you do something. It's about looking at something from the most effective perspective (or a number of different perspectives). It's about asking the right questions so you're not working with assumptions. It's about knowing exactly where you're starting from and being very clear about where you want to arrive. Wise strategy also involves answering the question: "How can I achieve (x) with the least amount of resources, time, energy and disharmony?"

In business terms, strategy is a lot like ROI – Return on Investment. When I go strategic, I'm looking at getting the biggest return on investment from all of the steps that I take. I want more bang for my buck. I want to have fun, not just avoid discomfort, suffering, pain and frustration.

I want to use my marvelous mind so effectively that my chances of success are increased ten-fold. I don't want to wing it. I don't want to just hope it all works out. I don't want to leave my life in the hands of fate. I want to be the creator of my success and have the life I most desire to experience. Forget being tossed around in the storm of life, praying to get stranded on an island that's actually habitable.

Of course, you can choose to live life on the edge like that. But why? The stress alone can take years off your life. So I'm going to make a huge assumption here and say you're probably not interested in winging it, otherwise you wouldn't be this far in the book. And if you're this far on the book you're in the top 10 percent of doers showing up and doing the work to attain authentic success. So, for starters, well done you.

In the next eight chapters, I'm going to share specific strategies I employ that support the Eight Pillars of the Authentic Success, which are: 1) Daily Positive Emotions (aka: Daily Joy), 2) high quality relationships, 3) feeling connected, 4) growing (personal evolution), 5) meaningful life goals (making a difference), 6) financial flow, 7) aligning with authentic self and 8) optimum health and vitality.

Nothing I share is set in stone. Everybody is different and there are hundreds of different ways to achieve a specific result. Maybe some of my strategies will resonate with you and you'll put them into play immediately. Maybe you'll take pieces of my strategies and add your own elements. Or maybe my strategies will cause a bolt of lightning to fire in your brain and you'll see a whole new way of doing things.

My aim is to help you get started, break up any inertia in your life, create a powerful forward momentum and save you time, effort and pain along the way by providing the actions, tips, tools and strategies which have the highest return on the investment of your time.

I also want to help you tap into the magic stuff as well. I want to help you create the positive, powerful mindset that causes synchronicities, chance encounters and unasked for opportunities to appear. I want you to bump up against the quantum field and cause an amazing chain reaction of events you never even imagined possible.

And you don't have to wait on magic. It happens after you get started—after you've thought about where you are and what you want and purposefully taken steps in a particular direction to get where you want to go. It happens because you're priming your brain and activating the reticular activating system (RA), prompting it to identify the things that are going to support the attainment of your goal. It happens because you're taking purposeful actions in a particular sequence and, in the process, you're meeting people who can provide specific assistance.

People cannot help you if they don't know what you want. Lastly, when you make your intentions crystal clear to the universe, your thoughts and actions impact the unified quantum field and begin calling in the greater unknown. Then life itself starts to provide assistance.

Remember, knowing and desiring something and actually taking the steps to actualize that desire are as far apart as the two sides of the Grand Canyon. Only when you act does the magic start to happen.

So ... go do some magic.

CHAPTER 15
Daily Positive Emotions

Do you mind if I use the phrase "daily joy" instead of positive emotions? Just writing the world JOY puts a smile on my face. It's a whole lot more exciting than writing "positive emotions," which sounds like we're having a clinical session inside a sterile research laboratory.

Remember I asked earlier if you can consider yourself successful if you don't experience joy on a daily (or at least a regular) basis? I don't know about you, but I want to feel joyful emotions the majority of the time. If I'm not, it's an indicator to me that there's work to be done and some changes to be made!

Of course, there are going to be times when you feel sad, angry, stressed, crappy, flat, overwhelmed, etcetera. These are all valid and inevitable emotions we all feel. But we shouldn't be feeling them the majority of the time. Right? And if it seems a little much to expect to feel joy everyday, how about setting a goal to experience joy at least five times as much as you experience feeling like crap? Yes I know—not very scientific. But you catch my drift.

So let's get practical and check out some strategies to help us achieve that. But first I want to expound a little about what/who we really are and how life really is before we get into the "negative" emotions that might get in the way of your joy show.

Energetic harmony

Positive and negative are simply two sides of the same coin of energy. When the Big Bang occurred almost eight billion years ago, the very first "things" that came into existence in less than .00000001 second were positrons and electrons—the positive and negative forces that make up the foundation of all life in the multiverse. Nothing would exist without these two forces that are ultimately not opposite forces at all. Rather they are *complementary* forces in the unified quantum field of existence.

You can't have one without the other. Also known as the yin (negative) and yang (positive) elements of creation, electrons and positrons act as one even though they "show up" as distinctly separate particles. As one, these complementary forces provide the balance and harmony needed for life to occur. Yes, it sounds woo-woo, but it's really just science.

At the level of biochemistry (meaning our humanity), positive and negative energies show up as male (yang) and female (yin). Dr John Demartini, a specialist and researcher in human behavior, says at our essence at the quantum level we are energy beings living in an entire universe of pure energy. When we're harmonized and truly balanced we are pure light and love. This is the natural state of our energetic selves.

At the level of human emotions we have positive and negative feelings that, when balanced, bring us to a state where we are energetically harmonized and capable of expressing as whole beings. The "ideal emotional state" doesn't have excessive highs or excessive lows. It's a state of equanimity. Bouncing out of your skin and constantly on a high isn't healthy because it isn't balanced and thus can't be sustained. Worse, excessive highs always demand to be balanced out by excessive lows. Manic depression is always balanced by manic highs.

The ideal state is a state of pure harmony—what I call "joy." The Buddha called it "the middle way." No matter what you call it, there is a deep sense of fulfillment. When you see pictures of the Dalai Lama, regardless of whether he's smiling or not, he looks serene. I actually had the privilege of seeing him in Sun Valley (USA) back in 2005. It was a magical experience, which I won't ever forget. Apart from being the funniest guy ever (everyone in the audience laughed so much), the best way to describe him is as a total lightness of being. He was pure harmony—so much so that his harmony infused the thousand plus people that were there to hear him talk.

In *The Book of Joy*, which he wrote with Archbishop Desmond Tutu, the Dalai Lama clearly states that if he hadn't had the experience of suffering through his exile and over the treatment of the Tibetan people, he wouldn't have experienced the joy that came with the experiences either. It's not just that we need to experience some pain, setbacks, disappointment and discomfort to appreciate the good times. It seems we have to move through negative experiences to fully experience joy in all of its richness.

Most people, if asked if they'd like to be hooked up to a machine that kept them happy 24/7, soon realize that although being happy all the time might seem great at first, it also might be completely boring and ultimately dulling.

So, now that we've looked at the Big Picture of positive and negative, lets dive into strategies that will enable you to get the most out of negative emotions and the pain they bring.

What's the message?

One of their main benefits of negative emotions is that they provide a very clear signal that something in life is out of balance and needs attention and correction.

Feeling angry? What needs to be done? Do you need to learn better coping strategies? Do you need to change your expectations? Do you need to speak your truth? Do you need to stand up for yourself? Do you need to let go of something? Do you need to protect yourself or someone important to you? Do you need to forgive yourself? Do you need to change your inner dialogue? Do you need to change your expectations? What is anger telling you about yourself and your life? What's out of balance?

Feeling sad? Do you need to cry? Do you need to let go? Do you need to get a different perspective from someone? Do you need to make lifestyle changes? Do you need to change your expectations? Do you need to speak to your therapist, minister, priest, counselor or coach? Do you need to rest your body more? Do you need to address abandonment? A feeling of lessness? What is sadness telling you about yourself and your life? What's out of balance?

Feeling ashamed? Do you need to love and accept yourself for what you did or did not do? Do you need to embrace your imperfections? Do you need to see a specialist? Do you need to spend time with your most compassionate and empathetic friend? Do you need to forgive yourself? Do you need to change your expectations? What is shame telling you about yourself and your life? What's out of balance?

Feeling anxious? What's driving the anxiety? Do you need to step back and take a break? Do you need to slow down? Do you need to modify your expectations? Do you need a different perspective? Do you need help? Do you need to draw on other resources? Do you need to get clear on the full picture? Do you need to verify any assumptions you are making? Do you need to modify your goals? Do you need to accept that there will always be some fear doing new things and move forward anyway? Do you need to learn some new coping strategies? What is anxiety telling you about yourself and your life? What's out of balance?

Helplessness ... feeling worthless ... feeling conflicted ... feeling overwhelmed ... feeling unsafe ... feeling unsupported ... go through every one of these emotions and ask the questions, "What is this emotion telling me? What needs to be done?" All of them can provide a dialogue and tell you what needs to be done to balance out the negative emotion and bring you back into harmony.

The physical downside of emotions

The reason that we need to work on balancing our emotions and come back to a state of joy is that negative emotions can adversely affect the health of our bodies if no action is taken to bring them back into harmony. If we stay in a chronic state of stress, over activity of the sympathetic nervous system (fight or flight response) stimulates the secretion of excessive amounts of cortisol, adrenaline, and other biochemicals that can potentially damage cells and thus the organs and systems in the body. The immune system will also be compromised.

The solution? Be present with the negative emotion. Don't avoid it. Don't medicate it. Make it conscious. Experience the emotion. Hear what it's trying to tell you and then follow up on that internal body signal with some form of action. Start a new dialogue in your mind, or direct your awareness in a new direction. Surrender to the emotion and trust where it takes you.

Doing the turnaround

Biochemicals triggered by emotions last for short periods of time. For instance, imagine you see what you think is a snake. You go into an immediate stress response. The body fires off adrenaline, blood shifts to the major organs, heart rate increases, the digestive system is suppressed, the eyes dilate, sweat glands activate, etcetera. But then you realize it's a stick. In a relatively short space of time (5-10 minutes), your heart rate reduces and the autonomic nervous system returns the internal systems back to homeostasis. Maybe not as quickly as they were activated. But you do return to a normal state.

In this case fear was deactivated when the mind perceived there was no threat. Which means that by changing your mind's interpretation of events (past, present or future) your body will respond sooner or later, depending on how efficiently you manage your mind, by shifting into a healthier more normal state of function.

Unfortunately, many of the negative stories we run in our minds and the emotional experiences attached to them, can last weeks, months, years, decades, even lifetimes. See how important being conscious is? Being conscious—aware of our external and internal states—is one of the greatest ways to reduce the impact and duration of negative stressful emotions on the body.

Martin Seligman, one of the founders of *Positive Psychology*, talks about the difference between *post traumatic stress* and *post traumatic growth*. He explains how two people can have similar experiences and one is empowered by the experience and the other is disempowered by the experience. Same event, but observed, represented and remembered in very different ways, which creates a very different response in the body.

The stress response in our bodies can be turned on or turned off by resources we have at our disposal. We are ultimately in charge of the way we think, the way we choose to feel (yes, it can be a conscious act), and the way we behave. Which means we never have to be at the mercy of negative external (and internal) forces again.

Finishing on the positive

The aim is not to be completely free of negative emotions. That's pretty much impossible. The trick is to manage them and not succumb to them. Besides, there's nothing wrong with negative emotions. They're a natural part of life and very useful for us in our evolution. They're a great guide for revealing when we're off course and not coming from our heart's desires. Negative emotions can also stimulate us to do what needs to be done to become better every day at managing our thoughts and internal emotional condition.

Chronically chasing bigger and bigger highs to satisfy our need for "positive thinking" and feel good moments is no way to live. I've worked with clients who are so busy looking for the "big highs" they miss all of the small wonders that surround them moment-to-moment. This is why practicing daily gratitude is such a powerful ritual. It connects us to the smaller things that show up every day—precious life gifts waiting for us to notice. And the reason I call them life gifts is because the reward of gratitude (what I call love in action) is amazing from a physiological perspective. The biochemistry of gratitude is deeply healing for the body—as are all of the other positive emotions.

And now the how

In this chapter and all the ones that follow, I will always talk about the theory and context behind each pillar as part of the bigger picture of authentic success. Then I will get into very specific and practical actions you can take. In this chapter on positive emotions I want to remind you first that many, if not most, of our negative thinking and emotions arise because of the habitual way we live our lives.

We do things a certain way because we've always done it that way. And we wonder why we're stuck in a rut thinking the same thoughts and feeling the same emotions over and over again? Nature doesn't work like that. Nature is constantly evolving, growing and changing, and we need to do the same.

Einstein once said the definition of insanity is doing the same stuff and expecting different results. And he was right! If you're not where you want to be you must realize, *right now*, that you'll have to do some things differently in order to get where you want to go. Whether that means changing how you think or changing your lifestyle and behaviors doesn't matter. Unless you do something different, your life will remain the same. You will stay at the same level of success in life, and, most likely, remain unfulfilled.

You need to take action. So, without further ado, let's get down to practicalities.

Attain real joy by contributing to others

One of the most powerful practices to enhance your daily joy is contributing to the joy of others. Acts of kindness are not only joyful for the giver, they're also great for your health as well. David Hamilton, PhD, author and a specialist in biological and medicinal chemistry, says when we help others the good feeling we experience is due to elevated levels of the brain's natural version of morphine called endogenous opioids.

Endogenous opioids cause elevated levels of dopamine in the brain, causing a natural high, or what is sometimes referred to as a "Helper's High." The other hormone released is oxytocin, called the "bonding hormone," which assists with the lowering of blood pressure, a reduction of free radicals and the lowering of inflammation in the cardiovascular system.

Sonja Lyubomirsky, PhD, a professor at the University of California, Riverside says, "People who engage in kind acts become happier over time." Why? "When you're kind to others, you feel good as a person—more moral, optimistic, and positive," she says.

In a study published in *Clinical Psychological Science,* researchers found that helping others relieves the impact of stress on health. The study, led by Emily Ansell at the Yale University School of Medicine, recruited 77 adults between the ages of 18 and 44. The participants received an automated phone reminder every night for them to answer a daily assessment questionnaire.

The researchers found that those who performed more acts of kindness throughout the day were less likely to report negative emotions. They were also able to maintain their positive emotions. However, during the days in which they were not able to perform kind acts, the participants reported a decrease in positive emotions in response to daily stressors.

The Dalai Lama and Archbishop Desmond Tutu, both of whom have been through significant hardship, persecution, and even multiple threats of death, are known for their compassion, kindness and generosity to others. As a result, they radiate joy, lightness of spirit and a childlike playfulness. They state in *The Book of Joy* that generosity, kindness, and contribution to others is an essential pillar to our individual happiness.

Aside from personal health and joy benefits, the other cool thing about acts of kindness is that they're contagious. People are more likely to be kind to others if they have something kind done to them or even if they witness an act of kindness. Talk about a win-win pass-it-on situation!

So dust off your Girl Guides or Scout uniform, hit the streets and start performing random acts of kindness throughout your day. Compliment the check-out clerk at the store on their smile, their earrings, their name. Smile at strangers on the street and they are likely to smile back at you. Be gracious to a waitress. Let somebody in an obvious rush cut ahead of you in a line. It's not the size of the act, it's the act itself that counts and the intent behind it. And don't you know that "feel good" sensation will last well after the act has happened in the hearts of all concerned.

PRACTICAL STRATEGIES

Here are a number of specific strategies to help you experience more joy in your life on a regular basis:

1. Use your negative emotions. Embrace them. Feel them. Explore them. Ask them why they're there and what they're urging you to do. And then follow your intuitions and DO WHAT NEEDS TO BE DONE.
2. Be very conscious about the meaning you give to things. The meaning you give people and situations causes an emotional response. If you change the meaning you change the emotional response. So CHOOSE the meaning that best serves you and others.
3. When you're feeling negative about something ask yourself, "Am I making any *assumptions*?" (For the record, if you're not 100 percent certain of something, it's an assumption.) You might be feeling bad over nothing real at all. So get your facts straight.

4. Make the conscious choice to do things that bring you joy. Practice daily gratitude. Spend time with inspiring people. Read inspiring works. Exercise. Eat consciously. Play with a puppy. Smell the roses. Take walks on the beach. Do work that inspires you. Live consciously.
5. Meditate. This brings you into a state of homeostasis and harmony. It also activates what Dr Herbert Benson calls the *relaxation response*—the activation of the parasympathetic nervous system (the opposite of the stress response).
6. Do the inner work—whether that's reading books about wellness and self-development, or attending courses, finding a good therapist to help you peel back the layers of your personal onion, spending time in stillness to hear the inner messages your intuition and heart are delivering to you. Take time to go within.
7. Slow down. This will enable you to experience greater perspective and see the bigger picture.
8. Do acts of kindness as often as possible: Here are a few more examples to get you started:
    - When you're driving, let someone merge into your lane.
    - Offer to stay late and help cleanup at your friend's party.
    - Pay the toll for the person in the car behind you.
    - Make small talk with the cashier at your dry cleaner.
    - Let someone go ahead of you in line at the movies.
    - Visit family members you haven't seen in awhile.
    - Volunteer to run an errand for a busy coworker.
    - Drive a friend to the airport.
    - Give a genuine compliment to someone.
    - Over-tip your waiter.

CHAPTER 16
High Quality Relationships

While writing this book, I was delivering a seminar and someone asked what I mean when I talk about high-quality relationships. Great question! Given the high divorce rate in Western nations, no wonder we have to ask!

Most children are getting a less-than-great example from their parents of what a high-quality intimate relationship might look like. Which means most people end up with a range of disempowering beliefs when it comes to relationships of all kinds.

Now, I've had a number of intimate relationships in my life, most of which barely made it past the 12-month mark. And while some of them were absolute shockers, I can candidly admit I was always partly at fault when a relationship ended. And yet every new relationship I entered I would say to my new partner, hand on my heart, "You're getting the best Carl Massy ever." And it was true! I could say this with certainty, because I was always doing the inner work. I studied my past relationships and did my best to learn from them—figuring out what I did right and wrong and how I could've personally shown up in a more evolved way. As a result of all this conscious work, I've been with my amazing partner, Ferry, for almost nine years.

That said, I want to state right here that a high-quality relationship is not about the number of years you stay together. In fact, my core belief on relationship is: Relationships last as long as they do.

There is no set time a relationship must last to be deemed a high-quality relationship. This includes relationships with your partner, your family, your friends, your work colleagues, and everyone that you meet or interact with. My next book is going to be called *The Guidebook to Outstanding Relationships*, so I'm only going to scratch the surface here. But you'll get the idea.

Signs of a high-quality relationship

Here are some of the characteristics of a high-quality relationship. My focus will be on intimate relationships, but most of the principles apply to other relationships as well.

1 + 1 = 3+ The sum of two people is greater than the sum of each person as an individual. When the right two people come together in the right relationship, BOTH of them are better for it. Both people serve as catalyst and support for the other person, making it safe for them to grow into their full potential. Ferry challenges me to show up as the best I can be, and I'm a better man for it. She also supports my efforts emotionally, physically and mentally. There are even times when she believes in me more than I believe in myself. Who wins? Both of us.

There is flow. Very few things of great value come easily. They all require some sort of work. But a high-quality relationship has a certain flow, alignment and grace to it—like it's "meant to be." You're both heading in the right direction, fulfilling your lives individually and together. And you can sense it. In my relationship with Ferry I'm amazed we've been together for so long and how (relatively) easy it's been compared to previous relationships. This is partly because of the person I'm with and partly because of the person I've become.

Aligned values. It is almost impossible to experience a high quality (and lasting) relationship if you don't have similar or complementary core values. What are core values? Your ideas about what's important in life. Who you want to be, how you want to act and the kind of person you want to become. If your core values are not in alignment, it's very hard to be in synch. Your values don't have to be identical or have the same order of priority. But the closer they are the closer you will likely be with your partner.

A full love-tank. Of course there needs to be plenty of LOVE in the relationship! And we're not just talking the physical stuff. We're talking about the stuff that fills your heart. The more we feel loved at a deep heart level, the more connection we experience with our partner. And the opposite is also true. The more connection we have—the more verbally communicative and emotionally expressive we can be with each other, the more the heart connection builds.

Experiencing a deep heart-felt connection, we're the less likely to be vulnerable and emotionally reactive when the inevitable challenges arise in our relationships day to day. When our love-tank is full we don't automatically fall into a hissy-fit if our partner forgets to thank us for something, or makes a snide remark because they're having a crap day, or leaves dirty dishes in the sink, or dirty clothes on the floor. The love makes the little stuff less important.

I highly recommend *The 5 Love Languages* by Dr Gary Chapman, where he introduces the concept of the "love-tank" and also shares some very specific strategies on how to fill your partners love-tank up!

Trust. No relationship can survive without a high level of trust that our partner, parent, friend or co-worker, will do what they say they will and vice versa. We trust our partner will honor agreements that we have and they trust us to do the same. This could mean anything, from looking out for each other's best interests to being monogamous.

Mutual respect. A high-quality relationship includes a lot of mutual respect for the other person and who they *are*—not necessarily who you would like them to be. Honoring one another's individuality is vital. Respecting what's most important to the other person enables them to be honest and speak their truth, knowing it won't be taken personally or held against them.

Heart connection. In all high-quality relationships, intimate or otherwise, you feel a connection at a heart level. For example, I like to work with people for whom I feel a deep heart connection. This means I'm lit up when I think about them or spend time with them. It also means I have high-quality clients.

Positive bias. In a high-quality relationship the number of positive interactions far outweighs the negative interactions. According to relationship researcher Dr John Gottman's *balance theory of relationship*, for couples to stay together, there need to be five positive interactions for every negative interaction. Which leads me straight to this last point:

Tough conversations are okay. A high-quality relationship does not shy away from tough conversations. We actually need some negative feedback in our relationships to keep them healthy. If nobody occasionally speaks up in a way that might be considered negative, it means important matters won't be addressed until it's too late.

A high-quality relationship holds a space for these conversations to occur without judgment, prejudice or bitterness, and without taking it personally. In the right relationship you're able to say stuff that might make the other person uncomfortable (and you as well). The ability to have non-personal or non-emotionally-reactive *tough conversations* is a good sign you're in a high-quality relationship.

Creating high-quality relationships

One of my personal intentions for all the human interactions I have in my life, is I want the other person to feel better after having spent time with me. I want them to leave feeling lighter, more refreshed, more clear, more present, more conscious and happier. If you maintain this intention, then every encounter you have provides the opportunity to turn it into a high-quality relationship.

Do I always succeed in this intention? No. But I succeed most of the time. Where I don't succeed as often are in casual interactions with shop assistants, bank tellers and other service providers. I think the reason is partly the nature of the interaction. It's superficial. Plus they're not in on the game. They don't know about "showing up fully." They're just doing their job. But it's also because I get complacent and don't bring the same level of consciousness, presence, patience or intention to these interactions.

So this is my work: To show up as that high-quality person each and every time, even if it's a 30-second engagement. If we all did this, the world would definitely be a more fun place to be. And yet, that said, if one person is putting in 100 percent all the time and the other person is putting in 20 percent, how can that work? I suspect and have observed that it does not work well.

Darren Hardy, publisher of *SUCCESS* magazine, once asked an audience what percent should each partner give in a relationship? (He was talking about intimate relationships but the same applies to other kinds.) He got various answers from the audience, the most common one being 50/50—which seemed fair and equitable. But then he shocked everyone and said each person in a good relationship needs to put in 100 percent of themselves—that it wasn't about keeping a balance and counting the score on who was putting the most in and constantly trying to figure out, "Are we equal?" It was about putting 100 percent into the relationship, regardless.

If both people show up with that level of commitment and consciousness, magic flows and firecrackers are a regular feature because the universe is always in balance. It's very nature demands it.

Up/down, right/wrong, left/right, man/woman, happy/sad, smart/stupid, matter/anti-matter … the *Law of Polarity* states there is an equal and opposite for everything in existence. Dr John Demartini, American behaviorist and author, even goes so far as to say that all the "bad" things—events and experiences—in life actually have an equal and opposite "good" to them … if we work hard enough to find it.

At the same time, people are different. We all come from different life experiences and backgrounds. To expect two people to be in perfect balance all the time, or aim for that, is unattainable. Ask any tight-tope walker. They're NEVER in perfect balance. They're constantly doing a dance from side to side. The times they are in perfect balance are a handful of moments, not the entire act. The same applies to relationships.

Only when we give our all, in our own way, all the time, bringing our special signature and flavour to the table, do the angels sing.

Is it also messy? Yes! Life on our side of the TV screen is not scripted. Real relationship have moments and segments of brilliance. But there's also a whole lot of being all over the place. But hey. That's that stuff that teaches us and allows us to learn and grow. The real deal is a mix between a romantic comedy, a thriller, an action movie, and maybe even a bit of the odd (MA) horror movie thrown in. If your intimate relationship doesn't look like your favorite Hollywood romance, breathe easy. You're in good company and on the right track.

Conscious Communication

The day I was writing this section I attended a business meeting and there was tension in the air. Stories were being told behind other people's backs. Assumptions were being made. Emotions were running high. It was so bad I even questioned whether or not I really wanted to be involved in the business. Maybe I should just take my bat and ball and go play on another team?

But we had one thing going for us. From the beginning we'd all committed to showing up with integrity, authenticity and non-attachment. We'd committed to conscious communication.

So the three of us came together with open minds and open hearts and created a space of non-judgment where we could share our frustrations, state what we perceived we were, or were not, getting from each other, and clarify how we wanted the others to show their appreciation, value and respect for us. And because we came together with the intention of harmonizing the relationship by reconnecting to the bigger vision with open-minded, non-judgmental communication of our own truths, we did get to harmony. And it left us all feeling better—much better—than we had felt before.

We all felt heard, understood and seen. We felt respected. We also put clear strategies in place to ensure that things would never escalate to that level of confusion and mistrust again. One of the main strategies we came up with, which applies to ALL relationships, is we agreed to deal with things when they were at an intensity level of no more than 7 out of 10 instead of waiting until we were all red-lining at a 9.7. Because I guarantee, by the time you get to 9.7, your nervous system will be hijacking your body. Your consciousness will be firmly rooted in the reactive, emotional parts of your brain, you'll have limited access to the higher faculties of your mind and your creative genius—all of which means you'll have essentially the problem-solving capabilities of the smartest dog on the planet.

Not the best way to do business.

Some of the keys to *conscious communication:*
- Find a physical place of harmony (you might sit in nature as opposed to the kitchen where you normally do your fighting)
- Open your mind and your heart
- Leave your judgments out of the circle
- Breathe deeply and calmly
- Speak your truth (get stuff off your chest) in an unemotional way
- Stick to facts and don't make assumptions
- Be 100 percent present
- Listen as opposed to hear
- Accept that *you don't know what you don't know*
- Own your own shit (aka take personal responsibility) and skip the blame game
- Stay aware of the bigger picture
- Look to the future (don't wallow in the past)
- Honor and accept the humanness (imperfections) in yourself and others
- Don't take things personally (that's the ego taking over)
- Be okay with being wrong (everybody is sometimes!)
- Be gracious being right (no *"I told you so's!"*)

Memories are faulty things

Here's one final important piece to this conversation. Extensive research shows that OUR MEMORIES ARE RARELY THE WHOLE TRUTH. The brain receives approximately 11 million bits of sensory data per second. But it only takes 50 bits of data per second to operate as a normally functioning human being. The brain filters out 99.99999 percent of everything through what's called the sensory gating system, leaving us with the bare minimum amount of data to handle. And the way the brain determines what information gets through into our conscious awareness depends upon our personal experiences, beliefs, and biases.

This is why police find witness accounts so variable and inconclusive. Ask ten eye witnesses what happened and you'll likely get ten different stories because our brains filter sensory information based on what we've been individually trained to believe is appropriate for any given event. Our eyes don't really see. Instead our eyes provide data that our brains then mold into something that agrees with our *internal* map of the world.

Bottom line, unless you're part of the tiny minority of humans who have a 100 percent photographic memory, don't fall on your sword over what you think you *know* happened in the past. Personally, I accept that I don't have accurate access to past events unless they're recorded on a video device. Which means I'm not attached to my memories. When asked about the past, I say things like, "The way I remember it is…" And if someone has a completely different recollection it's no big deal. I agree and say "We all have different recollections. Point is, what can we do NOW, in this moment, to move forward into a win-win situation?"

PRACTICAL STRATEGIES

Here are some practical things I recommend to help create high-quality relationships in your life:

1. Identify what qualities you most want others to display in relationships with you, and then get to work making sure you have it together in that department yourself.
2. Before you have a powerful conversation with someone that you care about or wish to get closer to or want to do business with, make sure you re-read the list of keys to *conscious communication* cited earlier.
3. Bring 100 percent to your relationships.
4. If a relationship feels too out of balance you might need to redefine the relationship, walk away from it, or get help to bring it back into greater harmony.
5. A Hollywood romantic comedy is entertainment, not a documentary. Do not buy into it or compare it to your own relationship.
6. Read and then APPLY *The 5 Love Languages* by Dr Gary Chapman.
7. Remember, you can be "right" (based on your imperfect memories) or you can be in harmony in a heart-based relationship coming from love.
8. Not only understand, KNOW, that high-quality relationships require constant energy, effort, and attention.
9. Know that high-quality relationships are worth ten times the effort you put in because they're the source of your greatest growth.

CHAPTER 17
Feeling Connected

It might seem odd to relate the feeling of connection to the idea of success, but answer me this. Do you think it's possible to feel successful if you feel alone—or even worse, lonely? Do you think it's possible to feel successful if you feel a sense of limited self-love? I don't know about you, but none of those scenarios would make a fulfilling life for me.

Basically there are three components to connection: feeling connected with yourself, feeling connected to others, and finally feeling connected to something bigger than you. All three together make life actually meaningful. A lack of connection translates into a feeling that there's something missing. And it's hard for many people to put their finger on just what that is because some areas of connection are very very subtle.

Three points of connection

Connected to me

Feeling connected with ourselves is about feeling connected to our expression here on Earth—the body and mind our spirits inhabit. It's about feeling grounded in our Earthly temple in this present moment.

For me one of the easiest and most practical ways I have to connect with "me" (my body, mind and spirit) is to dive deeply into a quality yoga class. Yoga takes my attention inwards where I get to connect with what is happening at a very physical level. I also physically and mentally connect to my breath—that sacred source of life we can't do without for even a few minutes. Have a little go and try this little excise:

Breathe in to a count of 1, 2, 3, 4.

Breathe out to a count of 1, 2, 3, 4, 5, 6.

Now repeat three times with your eyes closed. Let go all thoughts about the past or the future. Just feel yourself fully in this present moment.

Nice, eh?

Another way to feel connected is by feeling grateful for who and what you are. One way to accomplish this is by having respect for yourself as opposed to beating yourself up whenever you make a "mistake." Self-respect interweaves with this thing called "self love" which means when you look at yourself in the mirror you not only like the physical reflection you see, but also LOVE the intangible being behind the eyes.

In the book *Dying To Be Me*, Anita Moorjani relates her personal story about having advanced stage-four terminal cancer. Her body systems and organs shut down while in the Intensive Care Unit. As her body shut down, she had what is termed a Near Death Experience (NDE) where she had the experience of loving herself unconditionally. After the NDE, her cancer (which included tumors the size of tennis balls) miraculously disappeared over a matter of weeks and she returned to full health. Her lesson out of the experience and her message today is that the more we love ourselves compassionately and unconditionally, without judgment, the more we live in harmony and are supported by the flow of life.

This is what I mean when I talk about having a deep and meaningful connection with ourselves. It's not arrogance or vanity, but something more pure and life giving as opposed to life taking.

When we're deeply connected, approving, accepting and loving of ourselves, life picks us up and carries us along like riding in a big river. We have more ease in life. We experience greater synchronicities. We become "luckier." And we generally have a more joyful life experience.

Connected to others

Here I want to talk more about feeing connected to others that are not necessarily in your inner circles of family, friends, and colleagues.

Feeling a deeper connection to the many people you cross paths with through the course of a day in your local community (for those of us not living on a deserted island) is a very heart-based experience—a heart-based experience based in an attitude of being willing to help strangers in need, knowing they will help you if you're in need in return. It's about initiating or returning a smile or a hello to a stranger. It's about respecting other people for doing the best they can with what they have for now.

This takes work. I have to admit at times I allow myself to get annoyed— like when I'm riding my motorbike through the streets of Bali. People are always ducking and weaving in their cars and motorbikes with little regard for themselves or respect for others. (Well, that's the story I tell.) And my irritation cuts me off from people. I have to remind myself that many people riding on the roads don't have a license. They've never taken a driving course or a test and have no idea there are things such as "road rules." Remembering this— remembering that people are mostly doing the best they can with what they have to work with—I open my heart back up again. And because I no longer feel like everybody's out to get me, my brain relaxes and I experience less of stress response. And presto! My connection is reestablished.

The key is not to fall into judgment and close our hearts. When we do this, we cut of an essential connection for our own health, happiness and wellbeing. When we keep our minds and hearts open and beating with this thing called love, we become aware that we're wired into something much bigger than us—which takes me onto the last part of the connection triad.

Connection to something bigger

I rarely publicly share my spiritual beliefs because I believe it's personal and I'm not about to tell someone what I think they ought to believe. But this is important, so please bear with me for a moment.

When I was a kid my parents sent me and my brother and sister to Sunday School at the Uniting Church. It never resonated with me and when I was old enough I offered to cut our very large lawn for three hours every Sunday morning instead of going to church. By the time I got into the Army I was calling myself an atheist and squirmed whenever we had to attend a church service—unless it was a wedding. Then my focus was on the reception party to follow and the chance of meeting a beautiful woman.

It wasn't until I was about 30 and got introduced to more Eastern traditions of spirituality that I started being cool with the concept of there being something bigger than me and some sort of order to it all. Now 15 years later, I have my own personal spiritual practice and beliefs, tailor-made for me by me. And I like to think this serves me well.

In the course of my spiritual self-education I came to understand that there is something bigger—I mean MUCH bigger—like as big as, say, the size of the universe BIG ... the unspeakable force that provides us with all the nourishment and materials, natural and man-made, that makes everything possible. Call it the force of nature or the life force or the FORCE (as in Star Wars) if you will. Names don't matter.

For those of you who are open to the idea of there being something bigger and harder to define, whether it's called God, or Source, or Allah, or Gaia, or the Universe, or Spirit, or the Unified Quantum Field, or Life, or Mother Nature, or the Infinite, let me get up close and personal about why I feel connecting to something bigger is so important.

My thinking is, if we truly feel we're loved by Life or God or (fill in the blank with your own term), then this feeling becomes an actual physiological expression in our bodies giving us a physical sense of well-being. And because this kind of love is unconditional, it means I can be a dill, a saint, an idiot, a Marta, a dropkick, etc. and I will STILL be loved. And THAT is powerful stuff.

Which doesn't mean I don't take responsibility. It just means that when I make my inevitable human mistakes—even when I might stop loving myself—there's something much bigger than me that loves me unconditionally. And just knowing that makes me more courageous, more daring, more compassionate with others and less dependent on other people to provide me love. I'm less needy overall and more relaxed about life. And because I don't enter relationships with any need for love and approval, I'm all the more likely to be loved.

As Rich Litvin puts it in his book *The Prosperous Coach*, "Needy is creepy." All I can say to that is "right on." Knowing I'm loved unconditionally no matter what makes all the difference.

One last thing.

A few months before writing this section I went through a period of time where I felt somewhat disconnected. I couldn't put my finger on it or explain exactly what I was feeling. I just didn't feel grounded or hooked up. I also went through a short period of feeling crippling doubt, which was very debilitating.

Normally I can quickly move out of something like that. But feeling disconnected, my internal power source seemed to have gone missing. So I did a bunch of inner work and discovered that a recent incident had triggered some unprocessed emotional stuff from my past—which wasn't surprising. In my experience, if there's a disproportionately emotional and/or disconnected response to something happening in the moment, then nine times out of ten there's subconscious stuff going on and usually some past unprocessed emotions involved.

I also reached outward for help from an amazing therapist I use who practices *The LifeLine Technique*© developed by Dr Darren Weissman— an incredibly effective technique that uses muscle testing (kinesiology) to understand what's happening at a nervous system level. For those who understand chakras (the body's energy centers), I tested weak for my 7th chakra, which indicated a disconnection from Source. By working on the unprocessed emotions and by enhancing my spiritual practices, I soon began to feel centered, grounded, reconnected and free of self-doubt again.

My point is, *we only know what we know and we don't know what we don't know*. There's so much going on beneath the surface of things. And scientific "facts" change every decade as new information and equipment become available. Being open-minded and connected to larger possibilities serves us well because there are all sorts of methods evolving for discovering answers to our issues and healing them. So I urge you to please keep an open mind. It's the doorway for connection!

PRACTICAL STRATEGIES

Time for us to get practical with the best things I know to increase the level of connection with yourself, others and something bigger:
- Do Yoga. The real yoga, not just the exercise-oriented stuff. Real yoga is an inner meditative practice as well as a physical discipline. (Check out the great crew at *The Practice* in Bali!)
- Meditate. For how-to tips check out *The Guidebook to Optimum Health* or download the relevant chapter from my website for free. There are numerous other books and resources on the topic. Take a class with a great teacher. It will be the best investment you ever make.
- Pay attention to your heart. Is it closed or open? If you find yourself in a lot of fear, judging others, and being distrustful it likely means your heart is closed off and you've lost your life connection.
- Is there some internal story running (based in your past) which makes you fearful and judgmental? Be aware of how your internal stories and dialogue are affecting you.
- Establish and actively perform a daily spiritual practice or way to connect to something bigger. That could be prayer, attending a place of worship, meditating, or simply walking in nature.
- Do charity work. Contribute beyond yourself.
- Practice gratitude daily. Giving thanks puts us in a state that is more open to receiving and experiencing connection. Say or write down at least five things you're grateful for every day and then FEEL the gratitude.
- If you're not into spiritual work but feel a pull to investigate the possibility of a connection to something Bigger, dive in! Read books on spirituality. Read layman's books on quantum

physics. Speak to someone you believe has a grounded spiritual practice and see if it resonates with you. If not, keep an open mind and see what shows up. All the Eastern martial arts, for example, have a spiritual foundation. A spiritual practice is a very personal thing. Just because you haven't found anything yet doesn't mean you should stop looking. If you're open, the right practice will find you.

CHAPTER 18

Growing

As I mentioned earlier in this book, I was introduced to the idea that growth is a basic human need by the success coach Tony Robbins. His hypothesis seemed to make sense. But it wasn't until I explored it in depth in my own life and in the lives of my clients that I really began to get it.

During my own evolutionary quest I turned to one of the oldest and wisest of all teachers for answers: Mother Nature. And as I observed every living thing, in particular all the plant life, I realized that nature is constantly in motion. It's constantly evolving and changing form. I realized a plant is never stagnant or stuck in time. It's either growing or it's dying. But even in dying it's growing into some other form—like fertilizer—to support the next generation of plants coming into life. The whole universe, which is made of the same stuff as us at the energetic level, is constantly expanding.

Thus, I realized it's also human nature to expand and grow. It's why people who have enough money and enough success and enough houses, still want more. It's why the human race reaches for the stars. There's this yearning and need within us to continue to grow and expand the expression of our "selves."

The opposite of growth, of course, is stagnation. I don't know about you, but when I think of a stagnant pool of water it brings to mind a stinky, festering pond that's a breeding ground for disease. Not exactly a place we want to hang out physically or mentally!

But just as water can stagnate, so can the mind and the body. When the blood flow through our body stops or is cut off from a particular body part, the affected cells immediately start to atrophy and die. When we stop exercising our minds they become rigid and the neuron pathways in the brain become fixed. It comes as no surprise to learn that scientific research proves intellectual stimulation (learning something new) is associated with brain health and a lower rate of Alzheimer's Disease.

I've worked with clients who wanted to know why they didn't feel more enthusiastic and happy about their life even though they'd achieved a lot of things. They had lots of material possessions and didn't really need any more. And they felt a little bit down and lost in life. Immediately I zeroed in on their levels of short-term and long-term growth. I asked, "What are you doing in your life that's expansive? Are you challenged mentally, emotionally and spiritually?"

Most realized they were stagnating in their lives, doing what they'd always done, thus reaping a harvest of boredom, discontent, and atrophy. Hardly a successful picture.

Thoughts on retirement

For me the idea of slogging your way through life, spending your time and energy amassing as much financial wealth as possible so you can kick back at 60-65 and live off the interest feels so 1800s. And I'm pretty sure it's not very healthy.

Studies about life expectancy after retirement vary. But some, such as the Healthy Retirement Study funded by the National Institute on Aging in the US, have found that healthy retirees who work even one year past the age of 65 have an 11 percent lower mortality risk than those who retire earlier. The figures in the studies are fuzzy as there are numerous variables at play—like how much the person's identity, social connections, physical movement, and self esteem is linked to their profession. But the correlation between retirement and the possibility of an earlier demise is there.

My hypothesis is that those who continue to find meaning in their lives and undertake activities that help them grow physically, mentally, emotionally and spiritually after retirement, continue to thrive and enjoy their life. And those who bought into an idea that retirement is about sitting back and not doing much except spend their hard-earned money on material possessions they don't need, might be suffering from an overall loss of meaning and stagnation of their spirit.

I'm 47 years old at the time of this writing and for me the ideal is to find something in life that you just love to do and then do it until you take your last breath. I just love writing, teaching and coaching and see myself at 85, still going strong, learning new stuff as I continue to read and grow.

Are YOU growing?

Are you constantly pushing your edges, seeing what you're capable of? Are you stretching your mind? Trying new activities and learning new skills? Doing stuff you've never done before? I sure hope so!

Or are you feeling a little bit stale or stagnant? That's okay—as long as you're aware of it you can do something about it. Maybe you've stayed in the same place, lived in the same house or worked at the same job doing the same thing for too long. If so, now is the time to add something new to the mix.

Gone are the days where people stay in the same career in the same company their entire life. The trend is towards having multiple careers over a lifetime. Our current world rewards creativity and innovation. Sheryl Sandberg (COO of *Facebook*) says if you imagine life like a jungle gym, it's far more relevant and accurate then the old model of seeing life as a corporate ladder. Nowadays we might go sideways or even seemingly backwards (like when you take a huge pay-cut leaving your corporate job to start your own business). But, like a jungle gym, those sideways and backward moves are actually going to get us to an entirely new place that might be higher (or at least have a better view) than the ladder we were previously on.

So, try seeing your life as a jungle gym. There's no success in going higher on a ladder that leads to a place that doesn't interest you. See life as an adventure made up of twists and turns and ups and downs and ins and outs and highs and lows and be willing to mix it up and participate. That sounds more to me like a life well lived and it certainly ticks the "growth box" from where I'm standing.

Need some ideas? How about learning a new language? My Indonesian is embarrassingly poor and this is something I need to kick my own butt into doing this year. Try stepping side-ways or upwards or out of the job you're in. See what you can achieve creatively in a different field. Start a side business and see if you can grow it into being your main gig. Learn to play a musical instrument. You don't need to perform on stage (unless that's your dream!). Just learn it as an active form of meditation and a stoker of your joy fire. Expand your cultural knowledge by taking a round-the-world trip or a trip to another continent and culture.

Maybe you want to grow in service? Think how can you contribute more to your local community. Or maybe you can help people in less fortunate circumstances. Evolve your mind and your life by studying a new subject through reading, through online courses, or through formal training institutions. Start a podcast interviewing experts in a field you're interested in. Behaviorist and author Dr Demartini says if you dedicate 30 minutes a day to learning a specific topic, within seven years you'll be a world authority. Just imagine the possibilities!

So, I ask you again. Are you growing in your own life? Or is there something you need to do to expand your mental capability, increase your knowledge, grow your intellect, expand your emotional capacity, and deepen your spiritual awareness and understanding?

PRACTICAL STRATEGIES

Here's a practical approach to ensuring that you're growing in all parts of your life:
1. Write down the answers or deeply contemplate the following questions:
   a. How could I grow more PHYSICALLY this year?
   b. How could I grow more MENTALLY this year?
   c. How could I grow more EMOTIONALLY this year?
   d. How could I grow more SPIRITUALLY this year?
2. Commit to do one thing in each category (starting on a small or big scale depending on your temperament) in the coming week.
3. Check out the remaining seven pillars to Authentic Success and personally determine which of the pillars need the most work. Then take some action to initiate growth in that area.

CHAPTER 19
Living a Life of Purpose

When you feel deeply and authentically successful, you know at a whole-body level that what you're doing is what you're truly meant to be doing with this precious life of yours. You're living a life of purpose, headed towards your uniquely meaningful goals

What is a purposeful life? Here's my definition:

A life spent fully and boldly expressing my authentic and unique self in a way that causes me to fully expand into my true potential in a way that serves others and serves the greater good.

Of the seven billion plus people on the planet there's no one exactly like you. There might be people with similarities, but no one is exactly the same. Even your fingerprints—that tiny .1 percent of your body—are unique. Taken altogether, your experiences and genetics, your thoughts and dreams and abilities make you special beyond imagining. So, next time someone tells you that you are "one in a million," thank them and say, "You know, it's more exact to say I'm one in 7,000 million."

No doubt about it, you are a gift to the planet. BUT ... you're only a gift if you come into alignment with your singular abilities and learn how to express them in ways that serve you and serve others and the greater good. Doing that is the key to living a fulfilled life and raising the consciousness of the planet.

Mahatma Gandhi once said, "Happiness is when what you think, what you say, and what you do are in harmony." And this changes as you go through life. As we saw in the last chapter, a healthy person in mind, body, and spirit shifts and grows all through life. What you think, say, and do at 50 is going to be vastly different from what you think, say, and do at 19—or 89. But we can have this feeling of harmony, this feeling of alignment with our truest best self, throughout our lives.

Flow

Mihaly Csíkszentmihályi (who probably terrifies people that have to introduce him by name) calls this ongoing alignment "flow." (It's also the name of his book.) Are you in the flow? Here are his six signposts:
1. Intense and focused concentration on the present moment
2. Merging of action and awareness
3. A loss of reflective self-consciousness
4. A sense of personal control or agency over the situation or activity
5. A distortion of temporal experience, one's subjective experience of time is altered
6. Experience of the activity as intrinsically rewarding, also referred to as autotelic experience

Flow can't happen unless we're engaged in something that is deeply meaningful at a core level. If you're not shy of spirituality it might be described as acting on a "spiritual calling" —something your heart and soul yearn to do and express … something that is greater than yourself that leaves a positive legacy. Something that makes a difference. It also can't happen without there being a certain alignment with nature.

As much as we'd like to think ourselves above it, we are part of nature. His Royal Highness the Prince of Wales (aka Prince Charles) wrote a book titled *Harmony*—a fascinating exploration into the history and relationship between man, technology, and planet Earth. Basically he points out that being in harmony with nature is essential for our wellbeing, our equanimity, our harmony and therefore our deeper sense of success.

Personally, I believe it's really hard for someone to feel deeply happy and in harmony in life if their goals and life work have a negative impact on the planet. After all, we're connected to the planet via every breath we take. And the choices we make today affect the health and wellbeing of our children and their children's children.

The biggest challenge

Around the time I wrote this chapter I made a decision to step out of my established comfort zone to become a co-owner at *The Practice* yoga center in Bali. Up until that point, I was totally on my own doing business consulting and coaching. I'd never really considered running a physical business or having partners.

And yet yoga had been an enormous part of my life since I was first introduced to it in 1999. It was a major tool I used for personal transformation. One of the key business philosophies at The Practice was the importance of teaching the practice of yoga both *on and off the mat*. This resonated deeply with me and I found myself talking about the center often—getting extremely passionate and excited about the possibilities of what it represented and how it related to my life.

But it was a huge change for me to step up and get involved economically. And the only reason I did so was because it was very clear that my personal involvement in this yoga center was deeply meaningful. It felt exactly like where I needed to be in my life—like I was on purpose.

Compare that to the way so many people decide to get involved in a business: "It's a great opportunity. It's in a great location, with good income potential, with a high quality team on board that can maximize profits." These aren't bad reasons to get into a business. My point is they shouldn't be the ONLY reasons. And they shouldn't be the primary reasons. These are all secondary consideration points.

Your heart and gut feelings about what's right for you must come first. When I was a security consultant to the Olympic Games, I was very good at it. I was compensated extremely well, got plenty of holidays, did lots of travel, and lived in some amazing places. But I didn't love it. In fact, apart from the personal coaching and strategizing parts, I wasn't enjoying my work at all. PLUS I had a call coming at me from another direction.

Is it easy following your life's calling? No. Just because you're doing what you were put on this planet to do doesn't mean you won't experience failure, pain, suffering, discomfort, embarrassment, ridicule, and a whole bunch of other less-than-pleasant stuff. In fact, all these things are stepping-stones to authentic success and part of what author and mythologist Joseph Campbell calls *the hero's journey.*

Every culture has its stories about the hero going after the dream and along the way facing numerous trials and tribulations before coming out the other side a changed and evolved person. It's just part of life.

It helps to remember that if you're following a calling and experiencing a lot of pain and discomfort along the way, you can still feel good and successful about what you're doing. You just have to remember to pat yourself on the back every once in awhile. You're going for your heart's desire. Good on you!

Remember Earl Nightingale's statement about "Success being the progressive realization of a worthy ideal?" Well, it is. Just moving in the direction of something you deem to be worthy should be enough to evoke inner feelings of success ... if you allow it and give yourself credit where and when it's due.

If you're doing something because *you are good at* it as opposed to doing something that's *aligned with who you are* as a uniquely special person, be forewarned: life is not going to give you all the gifts you seek.

How do I know I'm on target for a purposeful life?

Paolo Coelho, the famous Brazilian author who wrote the hugely successful book *The Alchemist*, was on the Oprah Winfrey show when he made the statement "Everyone knows what their calling is."

Oprah quickly pointed out that she'd heard lots of people complaining that they didn't know what their purpose or calling was. To which Coelho, in a gravelly and resolute voice replied, "They know. It's just difficult to accept that you know what you're supposed to do, but are not doing it." To which Oprah nodded her head in surprised agreement.

It's been my experience that we all know, at some level, what we're meant to be doing with this precious life of ours. The challenge is for people to take up the calling. Too often we continue doing what we're good at instead of facing the risk of embarking on our *hero's journey*.

I often work with people who know what they really want to be doing. They just have absolutely no idea about how to make it happen. Or they worry making a change will cause pain or suffering to people around them. But I tell them there is a way. There is always a way. The solution may not be fun or easy or free of challenges. But there is always a choice and a way forward.

Now, let's take what I've shared here and turn it into something practical for you to utilize.

PRACTICAL STRATEGIES

Practical strategies to connect with your meaningful goals:
1. Check out *Super Soul Sunday* on YouTube® and do a search on "Are You Hiding From Your Calling?" with Paolo Coelho. You might want to read *The Alchemist*, if you haven't already. I read it once a year.
2. If you're not following your calling now and you're unsure what it might be, think about what makes your heart sing. What would you do for free if you had no need to work? What do you feel called to do? What are your most passionate interests? What are you curious about? What is the message you want to share with others? What makes you come alive? What might be the destination of your hero's journey?
3. Once you have figured out what your calling might be, play with it. Imagine yourself doing it. Where would you be? What people would you call in to help? What steps could you take to start bringing your calling to life?
4. If you have no idea how to bring it to life that's totally okay. In fact, if you don't know how to do it, it's probably just the right thing for you. Speak to someone. Make a wise investment by talking with a specialist like me who works on strategies for life or career transformations.
5. Ask yourself "Am I doing what I'm doing because I'm good at it? Because other people want me to do it? Or because I'm being

called to do this?"

6. Ask yourself, "Will fulfilling my goals or dreams be good for me? Will it help me grow and become a better person? Will it be good for others and benefit the planet?

CHAPTER 20

Getting into Financial Flow

The reality of this modern world is most people on this planet are not financially independent. Very few of us could survive if we didn't have a regular flow of cash coming our way. Even if you're completely off the power grid, you're still going to need money to buy the things you can't make or produce yourself. So let's agree we all need money. And having an abundance of it can provide comfort and the opportunity for some very memorable life experiences.

That said, let's get into more detail. How much money do you need? How much is enough before it stops adding quality to your life and starts to become a burden or causes sacrifice in other areas? The money scenario, like everything in our lives, is best managed from a state of higher consciousness where we see the bigger picture and thus have a more realistic perspective.

Yes, it's great to have lots of money. But it's not great to lose your health or damage your relationships or have no time to do things you love because you have an excessive, unbalanced focus on wealth generation. Money cannot buy or replace these things. Which brings us back to perspective and the consciousness conversation.

The amount of money you earn does not correlate to your level of happiness. One person may be earning $250,000 a year but spending

$300,000 and be pretty stressed out as his/her credit card debt continues to creep upwards. Another person may be earning $60,000 a year and live quite happily because their value system includes leaving a small environmental footprint and having plenty of time to spend with their family.

There are too many lifestyle factors involved to be able to determine the "right" amount of money that will correlate to a high level of happiness for you. Different lifestyles and different people require different amounts. Plus, the cost of living in different geographic areas varies widely.

One of the reasons I consciously chose to live in Asia (apart from loving the fact that I'm average height here as opposed to "short" back in Australia) is because I can have a more interesting, adventurous, and healthy lifestyle on a lot less money. I eat great food, eat out a lot, get weekly massages, work less hours from a home office, travel abroad and experience a whole new culture at about a quarter of the cost of what the same lifestyle would run me in Australia.

With computer technologies and telecommuting we're no longer restricted as to where we live and what we do in this modern world. Now is a great time to be alive and thinking (and living) outside the box.

Financial flow

I use the words *"financial flow"* for a very specific reason. Often it's not a certain amount of money my clients have that makes them feel financially secure, but rather the feeling that they have a source of financial flow available to them at any time. That is, the ability to generate income or increase that income if they so desire.

If you know you can always create more money as you need it, you're likely to feel very comfortable and content around the whole topic of money. If, on the other hand, you're scared about your continued ability to generate money (or be gainfully employed), then you're likely to experience regular stress around money.

What you think is what you get

Our income and our financial flow are invariably entangled in our mindset in relation to money. Our beliefs about money have an enormous impact on how we relate to it, how we use it, how we negotiate with it, how much we earn, how well we save, how far an amount will go, and how much stress we experience when dealing with money.

If you're not where you want to be financially, you need to work on your beliefs about money. Do your beliefs empower you, or stress you out? Do you feel empowered around money? Disempowered? Do you believe money is easy to make or hard to make? Do you believe that you'll never be rich or do you believe you'll be a millionaire by the time you're 50 years old? Do you believe money is a good thing or do you believe it's an evil thing?

One of the best books I've ever read on changing your mindset around money is T. Harv Eker's Secrets of the *Millionaire Mind*. Read it, if you haven't already. Start doing the inner work to change your outward experience and see where it takes you.

A powerfully insightful exercise

Write down "My beliefs about money are…" and write as many things as you can. Not just the things you'd like to believe, but the feelings you know are below the surface.

Here are a few examples of common beliefs about money: Money doesn't grow on trees. I'll never be rich. It's easier to fit a camel through the eye of a needle than a rich man to get to heaven. I'm not smart enough to have more money. Rich people are nasty. Money corrupts. Money is the root of all evil. Money allows me to do great things, etcetera.

Frankly, I'm more interested in the negative beliefs than the positive ones because these are the ones you need to work on.

Great dancers and financial abundance

I once had a client who wanted to be financially abundant. I sensed some issues, so I asked her, "If someone wanted to be a great dancer, what would they have to do?"

She said they'd probably need to go to a studio, hire a teacher, practice often, and continue to study and learn in order to be an excellent dancer. Then I asked her, "How many books have you read on finances? How many experts have you talked with about creating wealth? Have you practiced consciously using money effectively? How many courses have you taken on generating wealth?"

Her answers, of course, were "none" and/or "never." And her jaw dropped as the point clicked home. She's far from the only client I've worked with who hoped to become financially abundant while never taking any practical steps to educate themselves on how to manage money and create financial abundance.

So, step one in learning how to increase your financial flow and overall wealth is to learn some strategies. (I've supplied two below.) Read the right books. A great one is *Money: Mastering the Game* by Tony Robbins. He talked to the billionaires and greatest investors on the planet and asked them a powerful question: "If you could not leave any money, but only investment advice for your children, what would it be?" It's a big book and takes effort to read. But it's packed with good information combined with very practical action steps. He also busts some pretty powerful money myths. (Did you know most managed funds have so many hidden costs they become extremely ineffective for wealth creation?) Who knew?

The other thing to do is to talk to the experts (someone a lot more expert than me ;-)) and take a few courses.

Two powerful money making strategies

Before we get into these two awesome strategies for creating more financial flow, I have a caveat: Don't think something has to be complex to be of high value. Like Richard Branson says, "Complexity is your enemy. Any fool can make something complicated. It's hard to keep things simple." So get ready for simple!

Two ways to increase your financial flow are:
1. Add more value
2. Get creative

Adding more value

Einstein once said, "Strive not to be a success, but rather to be of value." And he was right. Experience has taught me if I add more value to the things I offer, I actually become more successful—especially when it comes to making money. If I give more than my clients expect, they're likely to come back to me for more business. They're also likely to tell their friends about me, which generates more business and therefore more income.

If you work for an employer and you give extra value to the customers, clients or stakeholders you serve, you're far more likely to be rewarded via a promotion or a bonus than the next guy who just plods along, doing the bare minimum of what they're asked. If you work on a contract basis this is even more important. The person who exceeds expectations by delivering more value than what they were contracted to do will definitely get their contract renewed—probably with a better financial package and maybe even a promotion thrown in to further increase their financial flow.

One of my working principles has always been to exceed expectations and add more value than what was asked of me. I've even gone back to former employers after five years absence and gotten consulting work with them. They knew I would add value to their project, client relationships, and overall business.

So ask yourself: How can I add to what I'm doing now? How can I provide more value to my customers, clients, peers and stakeholders? If you're working for an employer, remember, added value doesn't just mean spending more time on the job. It's about providing something extra—a great attitude, a new perspective or a new method for accomplishing some task. The more value you add, the more financial flow you'll create.

Getting Creative

A life coach I know says if his bank account is low that means he's not been creative enough. He knows the right creative idea effectively executed can cause a quantum leap in his income. So, when the coffers run low, he switches his mind into creation mode and lets it rip. After all, the human mind is infinite in its potential. When we fire up our frontal cortexes with intent and purpose, great things start to happen. How else did the pyramids, the Eiffel tower, the Mona Lisa, the Internet, and space travel come into existence?

Set yourself up for success. To be your most creative you need to be well-rested and well-hydrated. You need to be well-fed with high-quality fuel, not clogged up and weighted down by sugary, highly-processed, greasy food from a fast-food restaurant. You need to have a calm brain and nervous system. You need to be free of major distractions. And you need to create some space in your day or week to sit down and create. If you're running flat out on the hamster wheel, there's no room for anything else and your creative powers are going to be far less effective than they could be.

Consider teaming up with one or more like-minded individuals and do the brainstorming thing. Tap into the collective creative consciousness of what Napoleon Hill (author of *Think and Grow Rich*) called the Master Mind. Above all, don't keep doing what you've always done. Just breaking your routine a little can create the gap necessary for some new idea to slide in.

And remember: "Actions speak louder than words." They also have a bigger impact on your bank account. A creative idea may be high in potential value, but it's worthless unless it's put into action. There are lots of creative people with great ideas. In fact, we all have great ideas occasionally. But it's what we do with the ideas that determines the results we get.

Don't forget the secret sauce

Once upon a time I filled out the online *VIA Survey of Signature Strengths* (http://www.viacharacter.org/www/Character-Strengths-Survey) questionnaire (Created by Pennsylvania State University's Positive Psychology department) to establish what my Top 5 Signature Strengths are. The number one strength for me was gratitude. Since then I've realized how well it's served me in business and in generating financial flow.

There's an exercise I do in a lot of my workshops where I describe the following scenario: I've come into a little extra money and, since I love to share, I give a $20 bill to each of my three friends. The first friend says, "Thanks a lot." The second friend says. "Thanks," but gives off a vibe as if to say "Is this all?" My third friend says, "Thanks SO much. That's awesome. I'm so grateful!" and gives me a huge hug.

A couple of weeks go by and again I have some extra money. But this time I only have one $20 note. Who am I going to give it to?

You guessed it. The one who is the most GRATEFUL!!

The reason for this is simple: The grateful person makes me feel good. And I like to feel good. So I'll go to great lengths to give gifts to the person who is most grateful.

The same is true in life and in business. I'm well taken care of by my friends and clients because I always show a high level of gratitude for anything I'm given. I make them feel good. As a result, they like having me around and would rather give me the job and the money than someone else. In my business, I always offer grateful subcontractors more work and drop the ones that show low gratitude—even if they did a reasonable job.

The same thing happens with life. The more grateful we are to life, the more life rewards us. At a physiological level the biochemistry of gratitude not only feels great, it's actually been scientifically proven by the HeartMath Institute in America to be an emotion that creates greater energetic coherence between the body and brain. And guess what that does? It puts us into an elevated emotional state that facilitates more creativity.

Talk about a win-win. So, to increase your financial flow, start practicing more gratitude towards others and life itself.

How to feel more abundant

Ready for some counterintuitive magic?

Imagine how it would feel if you were so abundant you had more than enough money for your own needs and could give some to others. That'd be a pretty awesome position to be in, wouldn't it?

Well, guess what? You don't have to wait until you have tens of thousands of dollars to spare before you contribute to others. You can give $1 to someone more needy than yourself and experience the same joy of giving and at the same time experience the *psychological* feeling that you are already financially abundant.

I've talked about how the act of generosity and giving to others increase our levels of joy. So why not give to others *before* you've reached your ideal level of financial abundance? Wouldn't this condition your body and mind to learn what it feels like to be abundant? Wouldn't feeling like you have enough—so much that you can give to others—make you feel more successful?

Of course it would! As you create more success in your life, it benefits you greatly if you can feel successful *now*. So I encourage you to put this strategy into action and experience the benefits. Create the opportunity where you give a small amount of money to another person who is more in need than yourself. Let the act put a smile on your face and give your body a nice rush of joy and pleasure.

Bottom line, like attracts like. When you feel successful and abundant you attract more success, abundance and more opportunities into your life. Don't wait around for things to happen. Take action and condition your mind for success now.

PRACTICAL STRATEGIES

Here are more practical ideas on how to increase your level of financial flow:
- Educate yourself on how to create, maintain and grow your money. I recommend *Secrets of the Millionaire Mind* and *Money: Mastering The Game*.
- Spend time talking to people who are in the financial situation you would like to be in and get a measure of how they think and how they act. Draw on their wisdom and experience.
- Get familiar with the beliefs you hold about money. DO THE EXERCISE. It will change your life. When you identify a disempowering belief, develop a more powerful alternative and replace it. Work with a hypnotherapist, NLP practitioner or other professional who specializes in helping people quickly switch beliefs.
- Ask yourself, "How can I add more value to my current work?" And keep asking the question. Work at consistently upgrading your value.
- Schedule time each week to specifically work on creative ideas. Set up the physical environment to be conducive to creativity. I suggest starting with a 5-10 minute mindfulness exercise or meditation to put your mind and brain in a peak state.
- Practice gratitude daily. Every morning either write down or recite 5-10 things you're grateful for in your life.
- Turn up the level of gratitude you show to every person who gives you something or does something for you. And don't be surprised when you get given more.

- Contribute to others, so you get to practice the feeling of financial abundance now, thus becoming a vibrational attractor for the future abundance coming your way.

CHAPTER 21
Alignment with Authentic Self

Back in my army days, if somebody had bet me I'd write a book with a chapter title called "Alignment with authentic self" someday, I'd have laughed in their face. Now, many years older and wiser, I can sit here in my yoga pants and tell you it's one of the most important things you'll ever do to find success of any sort in life.

Ever heard the term "imposter syndrome?" It's psychology-speak for describing the feeling someone gets when they think they're a *phony*. Ever been there? I know I have. Maybe you're getting ready to deliver a presentation and feel totally out of your depth. Or you've gotten promoted into a higher position over the heads of some heavy hitters. Or you call yourself a surfer but know you're just a body-surfer and don't even own a board. What happens? You immediately spin into a freaked-out internal dialogue calling yourself names—and "phony" is the least of it! You look over your shoulder, afraid you'll be found out any second.

We all have moments of self-doubt. But if you feel full of crap on a regular basis, filled with doubt about yourself and your abilities to perform the tasks at hand, you're definitely not being your authentic self. Instead you're feeling psychologically and physiologically stressed, which makes the situation even worse. So, feeling aligned and comfortable with portraying the best version of ourselves is something we need to mindfully work on.

I've already shared my answer to the big "What's the purpose of life?" question. But here's another way of looking at it: We're here to fully express **the unique and authentic version** of ourselves, doing things that cause us to shine our brightest and expand into our full potential in a way that naturally serves others, while also serving the greater good.

It sounds big and it is big. I call it being the BIG version of you and me. Who else could possibly show up and leave a positive legacy? Who else could leave the planet and humanity in a better place? I don't mean we have to be responsible for world peace—although being the best version of ourselves, making others feel good about themselves, bringing ease to their lives, helping them be more creative, and taking care of the planet for future generations sure sounds like a plan for just that. Imagine if everybody showed up that way. World peace would be the least of our accomplishments!

So, let me ask, do you feel authentically you? Do you feel aligned with your authentic self? Or do you feel, like many people, that you're living behind a mask?

Get paid millions of dollars not being you

What's the difference between a hack actor and an Oscar Award-winning actor raking in the big bucks? The best actors and actresses get paid the exorbitant fees they do because they're successful at seeming so authentically their character that you stop seeing them as their true self and see them as the character they're portraying. They project an image so vastly different from who they are as a person, you find it hard to believe the transformation. Think of the late great Heath Ledger in his role as The Joker, or Jack Nicholson in various roles (*A Few Good Men* or *One Flew Over the Cuckoo's Nest* or *The Shining*), or Charlize Theron in *Monster* as a serial killer, or Meryl Streep—take your pick of her many roles.

These actors get paid a lot of money because it's really hard to completely assume the persona of a fictitious character in a way that's authentic and believable. Getting into and out of character between the movie set and their personal life is extremely taxing. What's the message here? *It takes a lot of work to be someone that you're not.*

So, stop doing it for free!! Especially considering it's having a negative impact on your physical, mental, and emotional health.

It takes much less energy to be you, to speak from your heart, to speak from your truth—to say what you have to say, based not on what you think other people want to hear, but based on what feels right or true to you. Not only does it take less energy—being authentically you actually FEEDS you and makes you stronger and happier.

Being courageously you, regardless of the audience or people that you're with, showing up as your unapologetic self at your imperfect best is amazingly healthy and satisfying. Exhilarating even.

The projection of a false you is fragile. This make-believe self is more easily affected by the energy of different people and things around you. It's exhausting to uphold. Plus, if you're living a false projection, it makes it harder for people to trust you. Duh! You're not being real. Why would they trust you? Why would you trust yourself?

Too often we're under a false impression that other people want us to be someone other than ourselves, when the truth is, people are hungry for authenticity. When you show up as your authentic self, approving and accepting of yourself, your light burns a lot brighter. People are drawn to you like a moth to a flame.

The downside of not being you

During a retreat I hosted, I had the opportunity to learn a valuable lesson about the authentic self from an attractive, intelligent, and capable professional woman. Just looking at her it was obvious she was successful in terms of her financial position, lifestyle, and the respect she commanded in her industry. And yet, one of the things she shared with us was how she felt she needed to behave as someone she was not in her male ego-dominated profession in order to operate effectively and keep things at a professional level.

So, me being authentically me, I asked her what she would most love to do in life. That's when the cracks opened in her projection and she totally lit up as she shared how she would love to own and operate a small health café near the ocean. While she was immersed in that vision I asked her who she would need to show up as in order to perform the role of café owner. And she said, "me!" She could be herself. She wouldn't have to be distant from people. She wouldn't have to be cold. She wouldn't have to be guarded. She wouldn't have to suppress her femininity. She could be her authentic and unapologetic self.

I don't know what happened to her—if she followed the dream and allowed herself to be in alignment with her BIG authentic self, following the path that was right for her. I truly hope so. That's my desire for everyone—including you.

So, go do what makes your heart sing. Do what feels right from the inside out. Drop everyone else's idea of who they think you *should* be and what you should be doing with your life. Be you. And be you in the biggest way you know how!!

Now, lets get practical.

PRACTICAL STRATEGIES

Practical things to become more aligned with your authentic self:
1. Embrace your imperfections and step into vulnerability, "the birthplace of courage" according author and teacher Brené Brown. (I highly recommend you check out Brené Brown's TED Talk on vulnerability).
2. Speak your truth. Be totally honest with yourself and others. Speak from your heart. The best way to do this is to start a sentence with, "What I am feeling now is…" No one can dispute what you feel if it's coming from your heart. They might be able to dispute intellectual facts. But they can't dispute what your heart feels. (If they do you know you're dealing with a loon!)
3. Choose your own path. Discover your calling. Peel back the layers until what you're doing allows you to be who you are at your core.
4. Stop being who you think other people want you to be. Be unapologetically yourself. And if it pisses some people off maybe they're not your people after all.
5. If you ever feel like an *imposter or phony,* stop and ask yourself "Why? Why am I feeling this way? Is there more work to be done? Do I need help? Am I out of alignment? Am I setting unrealistic expectations for myself? Am I comparing myself to others? Have I stepped in too deep? Am I trying to operate

beyond my skills and knowledge?" Answer these questions and then follow through on the changes that need to happen. Learn what you need to learn and then step up to the plate and swing

PART 3:
HEALTH AND VITALITY

CHAPTER 22
An Introduction to Health and Vitality

We've gone too far together and gotten in too deep to sugar coat or dance around any issues, so here goes: If you don't have your health, you don't have anything—least of all success. Got lots of money, but you're sick? Not successful. Got an amazing company, but no energy or vitality and no time to enjoy life? Not successful. Is this harsh? I don't think so. It's just the truth.

No one can enjoy life when their health sucks. Nobody can achieve their full potential and sustain it if they don't have high levels of energy/life force. You can't fully experience the joy of high-quality relationships if you don't have the energy to be fully present and fully alive. The health thing is super important to success and that's why I've busted it out as its own section.

Can I give you the formula that will guarantee you'll never get sick? Can I help you operate at peak form with 100 percentenergy all the time? Sorry. I'd love to. But our bodies and brains are more complex than that. One size does not fit all. The best we can do is increase the *probability* we will be free from disease and live energetically to a ripe old age. To that end I can give you some sound principles gleaned from personal experience and my two-decades of research into health.

I'm going to go into a reasonable amount of detail here. But for the deep-dive, pick up a copy of *The Guidebook to Optimum Health* if you haven't already done so. Ready? Let's go for it.

How much do you value your health?

Somewhere during the course of my life I developed a core belief that says optimizing my health and vitality is essential to having the greatest life experience possible. Nothing matters to me more. Which means I will never make a choice in life that compromises my health and vitality.

How about you? How much do you value your health and vitality? Don't just think about it. Feel the question in your gut. What are you willing to sacrifice to ensure your health and vitality remain high? What are your priorities?

Let me give you a quick example of how the health issue interrelates with everything else and why it's so important to understand your priorities. Here are my Top 3 life values in order:
1. High levels of health & vitality
2. High-quality intimate relationship
3. Doing meaningful work

If I make a choice about work that's going to negatively impact my health, then I'm compromising a higher value for a lower value. For instance, if I accept a work opportunity that gives me no access to a training space, no time to exercise, and no access to quality food, my health will suffer. Which means I will have compromised my deepest value for a less important one. Which means I'm most likely going to end up very unhappy … and less than healthy.

Where does health and vitality sit with the other values in your life? What is your number one value?

Using my list, let's say your number one value is *meaningful* work. That's fine. You don't have to pick health and vitality as your number one priority just because I do! (Remember being authentically yourself?) But you also want to ensure your health doesn't suffer. Right? So what you need to do next is come up with a few great reasons *why maintaining optimum health will allow you to meet your number one value of doing meaningful work*. For example:

I need to maintain high levels of health and vitality...
1. So I can come up with more creative solutions at work.
2. So I can quickly and efficiently handle stressful situations that arise.
3. So I can be a great example for my work colleagues.
4. So I can be highly productive.
5. So I raise the energy of everyone in the room, so we all perform at a higher rate.
6. So I can continue to take on bigger challenges and achieve greater results.

Remember that the bigger our WHY, the more emotional fuel we have to work with. We don't just want our heads in the game, we want our hearts in the game as well.

PRACTICAL STRATEGIES

What is your WHY when it comes to optimizing your health and vitality? Take some time to ponder this. Then complete the following sentence: The reasons I am committed to optimizing my health and vitality are ...

Write your answers down.

BRAVO if you took the time to do this! You obviously know the difference between knowledge and wisdom. After all, wisdom is only achieved when you consciously apply knowledge through experience ...

CHAPTER 23
The 6 Pillars to Optimum Health and Vitality

The 6 Pillars are about generating the health, vitality and energy to not only perform at your maximum, but to enjoy more of what life has to offer. You want to be able to have the choice to say "Yes" to a spontaneous adventure opportunity because you maintain an optimum level of health and vitality, rather than having to sit on the sidelines and watch everyone else having fun water skiing, playing tennis, or climbing Mount Fuji.

The *6 Pillars to Optimum Health* are:
1. Physical activity
2. Optimum nutrition
3. Detoxification
4. Rest
5. Mindfulness
6. Wholeheartedness

Pillar 1: Physical activity

Most people think physical activity is about weight loss, six-pack abs and looking hot in their jeans. Don't get me wrong, these are great by-products. But they're are not the greatest benefits to moving your body.

The greatest benefit is the physical and psychological feeling of wellbeing. When you exercise, your body releases chemicals called endorphins. These endorphins interact with the receptors in your brain creating a positive feeling in the body. No wonder people who run talk about "runner's high!" Regular exercise has also been scientifically proven to reduce stress, improve sleep, mitigate depression, reduce anxiety and boost self-esteem.

One of the leaders in Positive Psychology and a former professor at Harvard, Tal Ben-Sharar, points out, "Not exercising is like taking a depressant." And he's not kidding! In addition to endorphins, exercise causes a number of other beneficial hormones to be released in our brains. Provided we're not dehydrated or dulled by hunger, it also generally increases the clarity of our minds.

With exercise we also feel looser and more in the flow of life. Our metabolism gets a boost and we feel more relaxed while simultaneously feeling more vital. Exercise also makes us more resilient emotionally. On top of all this we know we're doing something good for ourselves and thus, when we exercise regularly, we build up self-love credits. And we can all use more of those!

Our bodies are built to move

In her book *Move Your DNA,* Katy Bowman says a normal person in Paleolithic times (Stone Age until about 10,000 years ago for some cultures) was physically active about 3000 minutes or 50 hours a week. This included walking, running, squatting, lifting, pulling, pushing, punching, hitting, copulating, climbing, hanging, dragging dead carcasses home and a whole bunch of other natural movements.

50 hours!! These days we think we're hardcore if we physically exert ourselves in one-hour fitness sessions.

The reality is that, unless our work includes physical labor, the vast majority of people in the modern world spend most of their time sitting on their butts. And I'm as guilty as the next person.

This means we all need to increase the frequency of the physical activity we do. We need to increase the amount of incidental movement (walking up stairs, walking to the shops, hand washing the dishes, hanging out the washing, stretching, etc.) and also significantly reduce the amount of time we spend seated without stretching.

The other week I had to hand-wash a load of clothes which included sloshing the clothes in a tub, rubbing the cloth together, hand wringing them to remove the excess water and then putting them on the clothesline. It was actually quite physically strenuous.

Ideally we need to perform more demanding physical activities at least six days a week. We need to challenge the muscles in our bodies, increase the activity of our cardio-vascular system, and support the cleansing of the blood via the lymphatic system via the movement of our bodies.

Pillar 2: Nutrition

There's so much information and misinformation when it comes to nutrition and how to eat to optimize our health it's hard to even know where to start. So I'm going to keep it simple. In fact, I'm going to start by quoting Michael Pollan, a researcher and author of *In Defense of Food* who, after extensive research, came up with this pithy remark:

> *Eat food. Not too much. Mostly plants.*

Genius!! 'Food' means not-processed. 'Not too much' means reducing portion size and overall consumption. And finally, for maximum health benefits, have the majority of your food be plant-based as opposed to animal products. That way you get the best micronutrients which are only found in plants.

My personal KISS (keep it simple stupid) advice on nutrition is to *remove or vastly reduce processed foods* from your diet. Once you remove the processed foods you eliminate huge quantities of sugar, additives, preservatives, artificial colors and flavors, synthetic hormones, and all the other stuff that belongs in the chemistry lab instead of your body. Eating real foods also means you get all of the micronutrients as nature intended them and the fiber your body needs for processing and eliminating waste and to effectively regulate your metabolism.

The consumption of a nutrient rich diet is more important than the percentage of fats to carbohydrates and protein. The focus for me is on eating a range of foods, which are high in nutrients and fiber. And if I were going to single out one substance to avoid it would be sugar and all of the bazillion forms it comes in.

Excess sugar is not just a weight and cavity issue. It adversely affects the body at a cellular and hormonal level as well. And it's not like you can simply dodge foods with "cane sugar" written on the ingredients list. When it comes to processed food labeling, manufacturers can be super sneaky. There are over 50 different ways sugar can be listed to mask the full amount in our packaged foods. Here are some examples: anhydrous dextrose, brown sugar, cane crystals, cane sugar, corn sweetener, corn syrup, corn syrup solids, crystal dextrose, evaporated cane juice, fructose sweetener, fruit juice concentrates, high-fructose corn syrup, honey, liquid fructose, malt syrup, maple syrup, molasses, pancake syrup, raw sugar, sugar, syrup and white sugar. And that doesn't include the more chemical-sounding names.

I lean towards a whole-foods, plant-based diet. However, I'm not obsessive about eating this way 100 percent of the time. Being too rigid in our thinking and behavior around food can cause additional stress and disharmony at the cellular level and in the digestive system. So very rarely I might have a bite of meat, poulty or seafood (usually to taste what my girlfriend is eating) and will occassionally let some processed foods pass my lips. But with processed foods it's definately less than ten percent of the time—probably closer to five percent.

I also prefer that a major part of my diet be foods that are "live" in the sense they are not cooked or cured. When I eat live foods I can feel that I'm incorporating the life force of the food. Not its micronutrients or macronutrients, but this elusive thing called energy that infuses our universe. Eastern yogis have been telling us for thousands of years that there's vitality in the food we eat and water we drink. So I'm all about tapping into that. Every morning as I swig down my green drink of fresh vegetables and fruit I subjectively experience that it's giving me more energy. Guaranteed!

Pillar 3: Detoxification

The sad reality is that we live in a highly polluted world—the most polluted it's been since the times of major volcanic eruptions in our distant past. Heavy metals, toxins, pesticides, herbicides, synthetic chemicals are everywhere ... we humans aren't so good at taking care of Mother Nature yet.

But it's not all doom and gloom. Yes, we're exposed to a lot of terrible things, but our bodies are resilient and adaptable. It helps if we don't live next door to a chemical factory (or directly downstream). It helps to be savvy about the clothes we wear, the household items we buy, the cleaning products and paints, the carpeting, furniture and flooring we have around us. Organic cotton, wool, rayon and silk are better for your body than wearing a synthetic material. Many companies produce non-toxic furniture, cleaning products, paints, carpeting—you name it. It pays to shop around and read the labels.

The right food choices are a HUGE part of keeping your body non-toxic and healthy. Organic whole foods can't be beat. Avoid sugars and processed foods like the plague. Make sure your drink of choice is spring water. Another thing that helps is keeping your intestinal tract clean and your gut flora happy and well fed.

There are more bacteria in your gut then there are cells in your body. Seriously. We have something like 100-trillion bacteria in our body—and they're a major player supporting our digestion and general health. We need to make sure we feed them the right stuff so they don't generate internal toxins in the body. And guess what? The healthy diet for your gut bacteria is the same healthy diet I recommend for you.

Physical activity assists with cleansing blood and the removal of toxins through the pores of the skin. Breath work is also extremely effective for increasing the detoxification process, not only through expelling toxins via the breath, but by the reduction of the heart rate and blood pressure. The calmer the body the more energy it can dedicate to health maintenance and healing.

Part of my "keeping my body low in toxins" regime is a daily morning green drink. Because it's high in nutrients, fiber, fluid, and already mostly broken down, it's very easy for my body to digest and obtain nutrients. This means my digestive system has an element of rest from early evening until lunchtime, when I have a bigger, denser meal. And then, later, dinner.

If you've been living the typical lifestyle, downing donuts and coffee for breakfast, eating at fast food restaurants, and snatching processed food packages out of the freezer section of your grocery store to microwave at home, I highly recommend doing a detoxification cleanse process before getting on a whole food organic diet. Detoxification of the body is much too big a subject to get into here. But there are many detox methods and programs available—including the one I outline in *The Guidebook to Optimum Health*.

Now for a short *green* message to close on: We are intimately linked to the external environment. The more conscious we are of taking care of our environment (aka: not polluting) the less toxic we will be individually.

Become a conscious consumer. If I buy foods that have been shipped from the other side of the planet I'm adding to carbon emissions. If I buy a typical plastic toy for a kid (that doesn't really need it) I know it's been produced with energy from the burning of fossil fuels, which adds pollutants to the environment. So I get them something different—a carved wooden animal or something. Nowadays there's an environmental cost to producing pretty much anything. Which is why I only buy shit I actually need and try hard to purchase low-impact products that have (ideally) been produced locally.

Pillar 4: Sleep

Once upon a time this was not a topic that needed attention. In the same vein that "exercise" is a modern invention, similarly, so are sleep issues. In the past people went to sleep not long after the sun went down and got up when the sun came up. We were in harmony with nature and the balance of our bodies' internal hormonal systems reflected that.

Today we have television, the Internet, bright lights, unlimited late night entertainment options, gaming, you name it. I'm not suggesting a return to the Dark Ages (though it does sound a whole lot more peaceful apart from the bit with the wars, poverty, plagues and lack of sanitation). What I am suggesting is that you be conscious of getting enough sleep each day because it will impact the power of your creativity, your solution-finding and problem-solving skills, your stress management and relationship management a bilities, your communication skills, your innovative capacity and more.

Sleep is a very important weapon in your arsenal of success. If you're chronically tired, you're not going to be reaching your full potential anytime soon. So follow the advice of the researchers and get at least 7.5 hours of uninterrupted sleep a night. You might think you can survive on less and probably can. But why? Wouldn't you rather THRIVE?

Pillar 5: Mindfulness

The thoughts we think and dwell upon and the emotions they trigger not only lead to different external results but lead to internal results as well. Ever been stressed and gotten a tension headache? Or an upset stomach? An ulcer? Nervous twitches? High blood pressure? Insomnia? Research in the field of epigenetics shows that our thoughts and consequent emotions also impact the DNA in our bodies, switching on and switching off certain genes, some of which make us more susceptible to disease.

There are numerous thinking patterns and corrosive thoughts that can cause a sustained stress response, triggering overwhelm, depression, the feeling of powerlessness, loneliness, mental suffering, and addiction, as well as an overall weakened immune system that can open us up to all sorts of diseases—cancer among them. But in this book I will only focus on a couple of them. And remember, it's not the thinking of a "bad" thought that's the issue. It's the long-term fixated attention on thoughts that don't serve us that creates problems.

Damaging thinking habits 101

Exaggeration

It seems harmless enough and makes for good stories. However, when we exaggerate our life circumstances, exaggerate the significance of things or exaggerate what's happening in our lives, we're also *exaggerating our emotional expression* and all the related biochemical responses in the body.

Frankly, the emotional stories we most love to tell are usually negative—how the boss screwed us or how our spouse deserted us or how our friend disappointed us or how we're financially stressed and overworked. It's about playing the victim and loving being the center of a drama that gets us attention. But do you think a small issue or a big issue is likely to cause a more exaggerated and protracted stress response in your body? Yep. You guessed it. Your exaggerated storytelling is actually increasing the level of stress in your body. You're causing your body harm, all for the sake of a "good" story.

Whatever the story is (or was), it's time to let it and your exaggerations go. Not only do I recommend stopping all exaggeration, I'll ask you to take it one step further. When it all hits the fan, try under-exaggerating when you talk about it. This will reduce the stress response allowing you to get more blood flow to your brain. Which means you just might be able to come up with a great solution to overcome, mitigate or fix the issue.

My personal favorite under-exaggeration is: "Hmmm. This is a trifle bothersome." It changes my whole internal response to a situation so I can deal with the reality much better.

Speaking in absolutes

Uptight, controlling, and rigid thinking leads to a rigid body (back and neck pains) and stomach issues. And speaking in absolutes is part of this dynamic. If a person says, "This is ALWAYS like this" or "It MUST be like this" or "That CAN'T be right" or "I HAVE to do this," they're locking themselves into a one-option path. Gone is choice. Gone is possibility. Gone is flexibility and flow. They've narrowed their focus, limited the power of their mind, and reduced their openness to alternatives. This is called being UPTIGHT.

The alternative to this kind of rigidity is to use more open-ended phrasing, such as "I believe it might be," or "I have a hypothesis that suggests," or "In my experience I've found" or "From my perspective it looks like … ." This way you don't have to defend your statement. Your mind stays open to possibility. You invite flexibility and new knowing. Plus you're a whole lot more fun to hang out with.

Become mindful of the statements you make. Are you backing yourself into a corner? Are you being a know-all? Are you being inflexible? Are you fighting reality? Are you creating a reality of limited or no choice? Slow down. Breathe. Open that mind up. Consider the possibility that there might be other options and perspectives. Remember, *we don't know what we don't know* and *only know what we know*.

Pillar 6: Wholeheartedness

I love this word.

For me it means courageously living life with our hearts fully engaged and fully open. It brings to mind people like The Dalai Lama, Nelson Mandela, Desmond Tutu, and others who keep their hearts open regardless of the adversity they're exposed to. As a result, these are the people who move us—people who cause us to feel more fully alive and in love with life and all its possibilities.

The first time I was properly introduced to wholeheartedness it was by Brené Brown, research professor and author of *Daring Greatly*, who defined it thus: "The capacity to engage in our lives with authenticity, cultivate courage and compassion, and embrace—not in that self-help-book, motivational-seminar way, but really, deeply, profoundly embrace—the imperfections of who we really are."

You can see how wholeheartedness relates so closely with the expression and experience of authentic success. It's the owning and expression of our true selves, without apologies and compromise. I love it!

Wholeheartedness is also about focusing on the heart itself. Not just on the heart as the most important part of the cardiovascular system, but on the heart as a centre for the emotions that flow through our bodies. The management of our emotions is one of the most important skills we can learn on the path to a life of fulfilment, meaning and optimum health. Elevated emotions like joy, love, gratitude, compassion, and enthusiasm give us increased energy at our disposal to achieve at a higher level, as well as change the biochemistry coursing through our veins, impacting us positively at a cellular and genetic level.

Unfortunately the opposite is also true. Consistent expression of emotions like fear, worry, anger, guilt, and disgust, not only make us very un-fun to be around, they activate our sympathetic nervous system in a fight or flight response that, if chronically activated, can lead to disharmony, illness or disease in the body.

I truly believe that if we don't live fully engaged lives—courageously true to ourselves—that we're likely to end up in jobs we don't want to be in, relationships that diminish us, and situations that require us to be someone we are not.

To live in a more wholehearted way it helps to:
1. Accept that you're feeling what you're feeling.
2. Accept that whatever you're feeling you're okay as a person. You're not bad or broken in some way.
3. Express your emotions in a mindful, loving, and compassionate way.
4. Listen to and follow your emotions—they're informing you that something needs to be done—take action.
5. If your emotions are too big, too uncontrollable, too suppressed, or too scary, it's impossible to move into wholeheartedness. If this is what you're dealing with, I suggest you get help from a professional. Never think it's a bad thing to get help—it's the *right* thing.

I have a regular therapy session with an awesome practitioner of the *LifeLine Technique*, which was developed by Dr Darren Weissman. I call this my monthly maintenance, dealing with emotional stuff before it gets too big or out of control. Other great techniques for processing emotions are meditation, journaling and Emotional Freedom Technique (EFT). Also known as Tapping, EFT is simple to learn. Check out the book *The Tapping Solution* by Nick Ortner for more details.

CHAPTER 24
Lifestyle Habits

The daily choices you make and the daily rituals you perform are a major determinant of whether you have a successful day or not. There are numerous blogs, videos, podcasts and books citing the daily habits and rituals of the most successful, productive and innovative among us—daily habits that allow them to become and stay high performers.

Working around the Olympics, I've ended up coaching a number of elite athletes. And I can tell you there's a replicable science behind the success elite athletes experience. They make highly conscious choices based on experience, knowledge and wisdom. Their dedication to completing a series of practical mental, physical and emotional rituals/habits before an event, during an event, and after an event allows them to perform at their highest level and establish a high probability that they'll perform at their optimum again and again. They leave absolutely nothing to chance.

Can you see how applying this strategy to your own life could have an amazing impact? In the Game of Life, no day matters more than this very day. Now is all there is. Yesterday is gone and tomorrow hasn't arrived. If you can become strategic and deliberate about what you chose to do at the start, middle, and end of your day, you significantly increase the probability of having a highly successful, fulfilling day. Practice this strategy every day and the sum total of your numerous successful days is a successful life.

Morning preparation

Do you think there would be a benefit to preparing yourself physically, mentally, emotionally, and spiritually at the start of every day? You betcha!! I've realized the way I start my day has a HUGE impact on how my day is likely to turn out. And yet how many of us stay up late at night and end up sleeping late in the morning? Which means we're consistently skipping breakfast, racing out the door, sweating it out through traffic, frantic with worry over being late for work … what a great set up for a lousy day and a lousy overall performance on the job and in life!

Compare that to the elite athletes, who, in their quest to create consistently peak performance, even go so far as to prepare spiritually for events on a daily basis—connecting with their higher purpose and the bigger reason why they're doing what they're doing. Getting up at 4 am and working out for hours every day, day in day out, at the same training routine, requires some sort of higher purpose to make it all worthwhile.

By creating an elevated emotional state they tap the power to overcome any real or perceived obstacles. They embody the power to perform with excellence and they constantly seek the mental clarity to find the best way forward. All of which allows them to slip into a state of flow with much greater ease when the moment comes.

Over the last ten years I've refined a morning routine that ticks all of the boxes for setting up an optimum day (for me), getting the highest results for the least amount of time with the least amount of energy expended. And it pays off. There's an incredible difference in the results

I attain when I follow this regime.

The Carl Massy morning routine blow by blow:
1. I sit up in bed. Stretch towards my toes. Then twist to the right and twist to the left.
2. I say a mantra specifically related to what I'm working on at the time 3 times (e.g. "I release the past with infinite love and gratitude so I can step into the future with love in my heart). This helps set the intention for my day.
3. I drink a glass of water with 2 tablespoons of apple cider vinegar. This is highly alkaline for the body and also stimulates my liver.
4. I go to the bathroom and while doing so I read a few pages of a book on health or psychology.
5. I walk to my office and stop in the doorway where I have a chin-up bar mounted. I do 8 chin-ups before I enter the room.
6. I then go into my office and meditate on a pillow I've set up the night before. I might also include an activity to process my emotions if anything is causing me stress at the time.
7. I finish by giving thanks for 5 things I'm grateful for and make sure I'm aware of the feeling of gratitude in my body.
8. I do a series of energizing stretches and movement for 3-5 minutes. I also say a number of mantras as I move my body—they become more like incantations in an integration process between my body, mind, and emotions.
9. I write in my journal.
10. I plan my priorities for the day, while I'm in a peak mental and creative state. This is a MAJOR key to success and productivity. All of the activities preceding this are preparing me to be in an optimal state to perform this one activity. This shapes my focus, attention, and intention for the day.
11. I almost always do some form of physical activity (yoga, cycling, dancing, martial arts, body weight resistance training or walking) for 30-90 minutes, but spend less time if necessary.

12. I drink another glass (or two) of water.
13. I wake up my partner and cuddle with her for a few minutes.
14. I have a green drink (about 2 pints or 1 litre).
15. Then I start playing the Game of Life.

Does this seem excessive? Maybe it does to you. But I chose many years ago to live my life by design as opposed to getting blown around in the wind, being influenced by external forces and people. It all comes down to what do you want from your life? What do you want to achieve? What legacy do you want to leave? What relationships do you want to have? To tick off all the Authentic Success boxes you need to create your life. You cannot leave it to chance.

And for those of you with super busy lives, kids that need taking care of, partners that need support, aging parents and demanding businesses—if you're sitting there thinking, "Are you joking? This is fine for you because you live in yoga pants in paradise on Bali. But MY lifestyle doesn't support this!" just hold on a moment.

My routine is my routine. It suits me. You must find your own. Remember being authentically you? But here's the deal: If you want authentic success you MUST organize your life—day to day—in a way that will facilitate your goal. That means starting your day out in a conscious fashion, attending to the needs of your body, mind, and soul. It's about finding the rituals/habits that deliver the biggest bang for their buck for you. And it's going take some experimenting on your part to get there.

In the *30-Day Challenge*, which is a deep-dive coaching program I run, we've developed a morning ritual that can be done in 15 minutes—a routine that can be expanded on those days when there's more time available. To be successful and have a deeply meaningful life, you have to get CREATIVE with the resources and time you have available.

Frankly, we always have time for the most important stuff in our lives. We always find a way to make it work. The same applies here.

If you're sure you can't set the clock an hour ahead in the morning to start your day off right because if you do you won't get enough sleep, then how about skipping the eleven o'clock news at night? Watching all that violence and drama right before you go to bed isn't emotionally or psychologically healthy for you anyway. Or how about getting off social media or the PlayStation an hour earlier and going to bed? Where there's the will, there's a way.

Finally, remember the safety brief the stewardess gives before a flight? What does she always say? "Put your oxygen mask on first and then attend to children and others in need of assistance." It's not selfish to make time for your morning routine. You're not taking away from others. You're providing a service for the people who are most important to you because you'll be able to take care of them even better.

About coffee

If any of you are wondering if I mistakenly forgot to mention the morning coffee ritual, I haven't. I enjoy an occasional cup of coffee in the morning. I love the aroma of it and the flavor. My choice, however, is to have that coffee AFTER my wholesome rituals. The reason is because coffee is a stimulant. I don't want to become dependent on something outside of my internal resources to wake me up. I want to exercise my mind and body and stimulate them to create an elixir that is even stronger than the effects of the coffee. My internal elixir is all-natural, has no adverse side-effects, and is there wherever and whenever I need it.

By all means enjoy your morning cup of Joe. But if you find yourself getting to the stage of dependency where you can't fully function without it in the morning, it might be time to take a big step back and do a more complete audit of your lifestyle and habits.

About those mantras

Originally a mantra was a word or sound repeated to aid concentration in Hindu or Buddhist meditation. Nowadays it can also mean repeating a positive affirmation or statement.

When I do my energizing exercises, I say a number of mantras because verbalizing and moving integrates mind and body. I say a particularly long one as I walk and breathe in place, swinging my arms across my body to help integrate the left and right hemisphere of my brain as I activate opposite sides of my body. The left hemisphere controls the right side of my body and vice versa, so I'm increasing activation of my brain and integration via the corpus callosum connecting both hemispheres. If we want to be creative and logical we need to exercise both hemispheres of the brain.

This is my mantra as I walk in place:
I am so happy and grateful now that I am ready, willing, able, safe, supported, deserving of, committed to and worthy of this divine flow of love, light, power, abundance, success, vitality, vibrancy, wealth, opportunities, connections, knowledge, wisdom, consciousness, creativity, compassion, courage, joy, happiness, fun, adventure, health, healing, harmony, energy and longevity into my life now, as I boldly step forward as the fullest, most authentic and unique version of myself, in a way that causes me to fully expand into my true potential while serving others and serving the greater good.

This mantra reminds me to step forward as the BIG version of myself every day—the version of me that's most authentic, unique and expansive, actualizing my potential. I guess it's kind of like my life mission statement. It connects me to the bigger picture and lifts me up. I highly encourage you to make up your own mantra and use it daily.

During the day

Authentic success is supported by living each day with awareness and higher consciousness and by taking deliberate action. Here is the list of things I do throughout the day as I play the Game of Life:

- I keep an eye on the end game. Where do I want to end up?
- I pay attention to what I am doing (I get present). I don't make assumptions. If I'm unclear about something, I always ask for feedback— just like an athlete communicates with his/her teammates and coach.
- I make sure I stay well hydrated to keep my attention, focus, and creativity at a maximum.
- An elite athlete knows that the fuel they consume has a direct impact on the quality of their performance, and I consume quality fuel throughout the day.
- I step back regularly to get perspective and then adjust things as required in relation to the bigger picture. I don't want to have such a narrow vision that I miss changes that may occur around me.
- Just like an elite athlete, I take regular breaks for rest. I don't want to overdo things and burn myself out. This one is definitely a work in progress for me as I can get so caught up in my work I forget to take a few breaths and a decent break to recalibrate my mind and body. In sports it's usually the coach that monitors players' energy levels. But in the work world we have to become self-aware and take care of ourselves.
- I seek advice when needed from someone that is qualified to give it—a coach, a colleague, a mentor, a therapist, or a counselor.
- I aim to do my best. I make a commitment to show up as the

best version of myself. Sometimes I miss the mark. But I just dust myself off and remind myself again who I am and what I want, and then get back in the game.

Bringing greater awareness, perspective, commitment, presence and consciousness to our days is about stacking the cards in our favor, doing the things we know will make the greatest amount of difference. And every little bit helps!

End of day

Athletes do certain things after their event has finished regardless of the outcome. What follows is a list of things you might do to wrap up your day in a way that ensures you're able to enjoy the following day in the best state possible.

- Review how your day went and imagine how you could do those same things better in the future. Don't dwell on past mistakes. Learn from them and move on.
- Re-hydrate with quality fluids.
- Have a high-quality mostly plant-based dinner to fuel your body.
- Visualize how you want the following day to unfold for you.
- Relax.
- Spend time with your loved ones and other high-quality people.
- Get a great night's sleep.

Outside vs. inside

Lasting change, such as a shift in our level of happiness or success, is rarely the result of external events. They can be a trigger, but it's the shifts that occur internally that make the difference. Even the occasional momentous event rarely changes our default settings.

Studies show that the majority of people who experience a major trauma or a fantastic event return to their former circumstances within a matter of months. Ever heard stories of people winning millions in the lottery only to go bankrupt a couple years later? This is why. Their external circumstances have changed, but they haven't.

How about that? The healthy choices you make each day and the productive habits you develop as part of your lifestyle on your journey to authentic success will have a more lasting impact on your life than hitting the lottery!!!

Certainty

One of our basic human needs is the need for certainty. It's part of our evolutionary imprint and related to our sense of safety. And it's not just psychological. Even our bodies love being certain of the environment so the nervous system doesn't have to use excessive amounts of energy staying on high alert.

In our ever-changing world, stress is a given. And one of the best ways to mitigate that stress is to have daily routines and rituals that ground us and give us the sense of assurance our minds and bodies crave. An effective morning routine of high-quality rituals allows us to start from a solid place as opposed to being buffeted by outside circumstances right from the start of the day.

It also helps to minimize the emotional effects when things go poorly. Routine is like a daily REBOOT for the mind and body. It allows us to start every day fresh without dragging yesterday's baggage with us. I know it helps, because I'm not perfect. Sometimes things just go to hell in this Game of Life. I've found, from personal experience, that establishing a healthy morning routine keeps me present and makes it easier let the tough stuff in the past go. Which finally brings me around to …

Self-love

I've worked with a lot of people, including the one I see in the mirror each morning, and I can assure you that very few people are a 10 on the self-love meter. What I have found though, is consciously choosing to practice empowering habits positively impacts us on a deep emotional level. The right habits cultivated in the right way are expressions of self-love. When we do them, we're sending a loud inner signal to ourselves that we love ourselves. Not in a narcissistic fashion but in a deeply caring way.

The body is highly intelligent and knows what's good for it. When we put awesome food into our bodies, we're effectively telling our bodies that we love them. And our bodies rejoice even before nourishment gets to our lips.

When we sit down on our meditation cushion and sink into inner bliss, our brains and bodies rejoice because we're lowering our heart rate and blood pressure, cooling down our nervous system and reducing our frantic mental activity. The same thing happens when we move. Our bodies rejoice because we're pumping and cleansing the blood, activating the lymphatic system to help clean toxins out of our body and causing energy to flow more effectively. All of these acts are like emails of self-love and self-care sent inwards. Every good thing you do for your body, mind, and soul is an act of self-love and has a positive and empowering impact on your psyche.

PART 4:
BONUS STRATEGIES

CHAPTER 25
Strategies to Serve You

One of my greatest joys and hobbies is thinking. And if you're thinking, "Dude, you've got to find more exciting hobbies. You live in Bali, for God's sake. What about surfing, or rock climbing, or canoeing, or paragliding, or rollerblading?" My response is that all those activities require props. Whereas thinking I can do anywhere, any time. No props required. I can even do it locked in a dark room being held prisoner by an evil tyrant who believes he's spoiling my day, when little does he know I'm happy, sitting there thinking.

Where am I going with this, you ask? ;-)

Well, here are some strategies I've thought about that will be most useful to you as you face different life situations. They will improve your mindset and make life more meaningful, pleasurable and positive as you journey towards Authentic Success.

Strategy 1: Work and life balance

Most clients ask me, "How can I better balance my work and personal life?"

When we think of balance we tend to imagine some perfect state of equilibrium. But balance isn't necessarily what we think it is. Remember the tightrope walker? If they're not balanced, they can fall to their deaths—high stakes indeed. Thing is, even tightrope walkers are very rarely in perfect balance. They spend most of their time leaning to one side or the other, using their hands or a pole to bring them back into balance. In other words, they spend the majority of time "out of balance."

What enables them to stay on the rope is their ability to make constant adjustments because they're paying *high conscious attention to their internal and external environment.* They quickly recognize when they're leaning too far to one side and use their tools to bring them back to center. They make micro adjustments so quickly and subtlety it appears as if they're in perfect balance all the time.

This is what we have to learn to do in our lives.

Step 1 - Know that you are rarely, if ever, in perfect balance between all the parts of your work and life and that that's okay.

Step 2 - Understand the more consciousness you bring to your internal and external environment—the more fine-tuned your awareness—the more quickly you'll notice when you're out of balance and the sooner you can do something about it while it's still a small issue requiring less energy to manage.

Say you're consciously aware of spending too much time at work. Solution? Make a conscious effort to shift and determine what specific things you can do to spend more time with your partner, family, and friends. Or maybe your health is being compromised. Turn up the volume on your self-care to bring yourself back into relative balance.

Have a big work project coming up? Communicate and strategize with your partner ahead of time and think of specific things you can do to mitigate the impact. Maybe it's a date night. Maybe it's booking a vacation or planning some quality downtime together after the project is finished.

The more conscious you are about the balance or lack of balance in your life and the more fluid you are, the easier this will get. And if you can't figure it out yourself because you're running so hard on the hamster wheel, find the right person or professional to help you get perspective. Come up with practical strategies to bring things back into alignment. And remember, taking action sooner than later is always the strategic way to go.

Strategy 2: Time management

Time management is not about how well we manage time, which is pretty hard to manipulate. It's about how well we manage ACTIVITIES.

The reality is we don't have enough time in our days to do everything. So it's absolutely essential we get super awesome at establishing our priorities. Which means getting crystal clear about the things that are most important to us in our lives. Once we do that and have the big picture, then we can establish what activities will get us where we want to go.

So often we end up participating in activities that are not taking us closer to our goals. Or our lives are so cluttered we're just inching forward. You must take the time to get clear about what activities have the highest ROI and do more of those things while ditching the activities that are not taking you closer to your goal.

One of my strongest beliefs (which is actually a mantra I write in my journal daily) is that we always have enough time to do what is most important in our lives. Our job is to identify, isolate, and focus on the things that are most meaningful, fulfilling, nourishing, joyful, growth-oriented, rewarding, good for us, good for others, and good for the greater good … and then do them.

Time management is about selecting and then doing the stuff that makes all the difference. This is aligned with the idea of working smarter, not harder. The best way to accomplish this is by asking filtering questions. Here are three of my favorites:

1. **Is this activity ESSENTIAL or DESIRABLE?** Always do the essential things first. This will reduce the things on your To-Do List by at least 50 percent. Because face it, most of us tend to spend a lot of time doing useless crap.
2. **Will this activity take me in the direction of my main goals or purpose in life?** If it doesn't, then it clearly does not make it onto your To-Do List.
3. **Is this activity good for me, good for others, and good for the greater good?** If the answer is "Yes," it's highly meaningful activity and should be on your list.

Asking these three questions will likely weed out at least 80 percent of the activities and opportunities in your life. Congratulations! You've effectively given yourself more time by kicking low-quality, time wasters to the curb

Next thing is to rank the activities that are left in priority order. After that, it comes down to personal temperament. Do you like to work things in sequential order? Do you knock off the biggest challenge first, so the other activities seem easier? Do you do an easy task first to get warmed up for the bigger stuff? Figure out your personal preference to establish what works best for you.

Consistency

I use these questions daily to establish priorities and weekly to assess my life's priorities to make sure I'm on track. I do not assume that because something was a good idea last week that it will be a good idea this week. New information or insights might change everything. Part of the trick to keeping balance in life and work is being flexible and realizing things—including you and your priorities—change.

Strategy 3: Creating more space/time for you

One of Warren Buffet's secrets to success is that he says "no" to 99 percent of the opportunities that come his way. Which means there's a lot more space in his life for the opportunities that he wants to say a big "YES" to.

So here's strategy number three for creating more time and space for yourself: Say "no" more often. Practice it right now. Say… "NO, no, no, NO!!, no, no, no, no, no, no, NO!!!, no, No, no, and NO!!!!!!'.

Now exhale … aaaaaaahhhhh. You just opened up a lot more space and time in your life to do the things that are most meaningful and fulfilling to you.

Many many years ago I let society, family, co-workers, and friends dictate what I should do with my life. They figured into how I should act, what I should be involved with, what career I should have, how a workday should unfold, what my career progression should look like. And I wasn't happy. So I let all that programming go. Now, I no longer should on myself. Now, everything for me is a set of suggestions as opposed to rules. And I can pick and choose what I want—what feels right and aligned with the unique life experience I desire.

I don't say "yes" to a party if I don't want to go to—especially if the company, food or drink is not to my liking. I don't say "yes" to spending time with someone if I don't resonate with them. In my work I consciously choose who I wish to work with as a coach—people who are self-motivated, who want to make a large positive impact in the world, and who make me smile when I think about them.

I'm okay with people not liking me (or even becoming upset with me) because I said "no" to their request. But this rarely happens. People usually end up respecting me more (granted sometimes begrudgingly). And if they do get pissed off it's usually because they don't have the courage and self-respect to say "no" to all the nebulous crap in their own lives taking them off their path.

So come on, practice it one more time... "No, no, no, no, NO!, no, no way!, Nope, nah, NO!, sorry I'm busy, can't do it, not interested, not aligned with my values, no, nope, spare me, and no friggin way José (that's pronounced ho-zay if you're an Aussie ;-).

A quick word on rejection

Turn around is fair play. Don't take getting told "no" personally. Remember, when you say "no" to someone you're merely telling them the thing on offer doesn't work for you—either in that moment or more long term in that it's not in alignment with the direction you're headed. So when someone says it to you, it doesn't mean something's wrong with you. Got it?

A "no" is just a "no."

And remember, in business there's a saying that "yes" lives in the land of "no." Some of the most successful businesses, books, and ventures, only occurred because someone did not take all the "no's" personally.

Colonel Harland Sanders (founder of Colonel Sander's Kentucky Fried Chicken) was rejected almost 100 times by different banks and investors. Now it's a billion dollar global franchise. The book *Chicken Soup for the Soul* got 30 or more rejections from publishers who are now kicking themselves because it turned into a global publishing empire.

I've worked with a number of actors and one of the most essential skills for them to develop is not taking rejections at auditions personally. It's just a part of the journey getting to the acting gigs—same thing for writers.

So don't be put off by receiving your own "no's." It's not about you. It's about the other guy. If it's not about them, it's feedback for you. It's new information for you to work with. Maybe you need to do something differently. Maybe you need to change your perspective or approach. Maybe you need to change how you show up. What can you learn as a result of getting that "no"?

Strategy 4: Slow down

The world runs at an ever-faster pace and we think we have to run to keep up. And yet to increase our level of consciousness we often have to slow down.

When we're moving too quickly, we're usually operating on subconscious behavioral patterns. In other words: *If you are not fully present, then you are running on a program.* And since all of our subconscious programming is based in the past, a vast number of our beliefs are out of date and not appropriate for our life situations.

Frankly, I'm a bit of a tyrant with my coaching clients about what comes out of their mouths. The words we say are a reflection of the thoughts we have about ourselves and the world—and they affect us and those around us. So often people haven't a clue that what they've just said is a piece of useless garbage they've mouthed so many times they're unconscious of it and have no idea of its impact.

If you say something enough times, like "It's to die for!" or "I'm sick and tired of _____" (fill in the blank) you'll not only believe it, you'll end up making it a truth in your life. It'll become a self-fulfilling prophecy. And one day when you're sick and exhausted you'll wonder why you seem to feel that way so often.

So please, slow the heck down and get super focused on what it is you're saying. Be intelligent and mindful of the things that come out of your mouth, because they create results—either positive or negative—in your external world.

Here are some of the more common dynamics of unconscious language:
1. **Making exaggerations** - Saying stuff that is not 100 percent true. The more we stick to the known facts without embellishment, the more authentic our conversations and communication will be. Which will change the results we get in life.
2. **Assuming that a belief is a FACT** - Our beliefs are not universal laws. They're ideas we think are true because we picked them up from some one or some book and then made them true via our belief in them as true. All it takes is one person on this planet proving the opposite of your precious belief for it to crumble to dust.
3. **Using *emotive* language** - This might help sell romance novels and movies, but it's a crap strategy to integrate into your life. When someone makes a comment like, "I just got thrown under the bus," when the reality is they simply got asked to do something they find personally uncomfortable, they're setting their nervous system up for a lousy ride. When we use highly

emotional words and evocative phases, they trigger a sympathetic nervous system response (the fight or flight response). The words we choose, or don't choose, determine how much adrenaline and cortisol (stressers) or dopamine and oxytocin (the "feel good" hormones) course through our bloodstreams. Our words affect our physiology in a negative or positive way. So stick to the facts and delete the drama.

4. **Not upgrading your personal software** - If you had a choice whether to run Windows '95 or Windows 15 software, which do you think would be more efficient? Same thing goes for you. Throw out the old beliefs and stories that served you when you were 20 years younger—"My mother HATED me!"—and update your software. What are you saying that's keeping you stuck in some old outdated way of thinking and feeling?

5. **Complaining.** When was the last time complaining made you feel better about yourself and life? Exactly. Never. At best it let you keep company with a group of fellow complainers and you all got to feel equally crappy together—which maybe served your need to connect, but not in a good way. The reality is, complaining has a negative impact on your physiology, your psychology, and your optimism about life. In the end, it actually makes you feel worse. Here's a great challenge from *A Complaint Free World* by Will Bowen. Set yourself the task of going for 21 consecutive days without criticizing, complaining, and gossiping. Not easy. But it's a highly rewarding exercise to go through. It took me about six months to make it for 21-days straight. This simple exercise really shifted my outlook, enthusiasm, and optimism for life.

CHAPTER 26
Honing Your Decision-Making Skills

If you're going to succeed at a whole new level in life, you need better decision-making strategies.

Decision-making tips

Tip 1: Begin with the end in mind

When it comes to decision-making, the most important thing is getting crystal clear about the outcome you most desire. Not just a little bit clear but REALLY REALLY clear. As the late great Steven Covey, author of *The 7 Habits of Highly Effective People* said, clarity is all about "beginning with the end in mind."

Here's a very simple and effective way to help you do that. Faced with a choice, ask yourself: "What outcome do I desire that is best for me, best for others, and best for the greater good?"

The clearer you are about what you really want, the easier it will be to discard some of the potential choices open to you. This is when you realise the difference between an opportunity and a distraction. If the choice takes you closer to your goal, it's an opportunity. If the choice takes you further from your goal— regardless of how wonderful it appears—it's nothing more than a distraction.

This powerful question elevates the quality and meaningfulness of your decisions and directs you towards greater levels of joy, happiness, and fulfillment.

Tip 2: Are you sure?

To be successful it's imperative that you work with FACTS not ASSUMPTIONS. Not only does it make communication better and decision-making easier, dealing with facts, not fiction, is crucial for doing well in the business of life. So before you make a decision about something that's really important, convert as many of those assumptions in your head as possible to *facts*. And if the facts change, be prepared to reconsider your decision yet again. Don't be a bonehead and stay stuck in a decision in hopes it will all still be okay. Be flexible.

If you're not 100 percent clear when it comes to important decisions and you can't get clear on the facts, ask someone *you respect who knows the facts what their opinion is*. That's just called being smart and using your resources.

Tip 3: Values matter

When we make decisions that compromise our primary values in life, rest assured, we will very likely end up unhappy. Which brings me around to something I call *Values-Based Decision-Making*.

First you need to get very clear about what you value most in life and then list those things in order of priority. At the very least be very clear on your top three values.

Now you have a clear map for decision-making. If a decisional path is likely to sabotage one of your top three life values, avoid it. As I spoke about earlier, my number one life value is my health and vitality. If I make a decision that makes me money (a lower value), but sacrifices my health, I'm not going to be a happy camper.

So your homework is to get clear about your Top 5 Values and put them in priority order. Then bring them to mind when you're making important decisions—or even a small ones. Decisions add up and small compromises can swiftly take you down the wrong path.

Tip 4: Slow down

Yes, I've mentioned this just recently. But "repetition is the mother of learning," so bear with me.

Let's face it—few of us will ever face a life or death situation where time is critical. I was in the military for 14 years, and saw only a handful situations that required immediate decisions. So, for those of us not in a life-or-death decision-making situation, my recommendation is always to s-l-o-w down. Breathe. Get more oxygen and blood flow to your brain. Drink some water to hydrate your brain. Have a healthy snack for fuel. Go for a walk in nature. Relax your body. Breathe. Sleep on it. Set yourself up for success. Create the environment that is most conducive to optimal mental function so you can make the wisest choice. Take the time to visualize your options. Use your brain and imagine the life your various choices will lead you to. And then choose.

Tip 5: Use your whole body

We've been gifted amazing body-based resources that have evolved over millions of years. So let's capitalize on them.

In addition to taking the time to set up the proper mental conditions and using your amazing brain, I recommend using two other powerful body parts in the decision-making process:

1. **Your Heart** – Your heart keeps you connected to your values and what you love. Listening to your heart guarantees you're going for the deeper meaning and consequences of any given situation. Ever discounted the advice of your heart? How did that feel? I'm guessing, not so good. "What does my heart say?" is a valid question I always ask and I expect a feeling response and pay close attention to the answer.

   Researchers at the HeartMath Institute in California have discovered that the electromagnetic field of the heart is 60 times more powerful than the brain's electromagnetic field, and that someone who is in a "heart-based" space can calm and entrain other people's brain waves from up to 10 feet away!

   They've also discovered that the heart contains a plexus of nerves (a nerve bundle) that can react more swiftly to situations than the brain itself. Which is why you might have experienced making an instant assessment about something or someone that seemed totally contrary to what your brain would have come up with—and discovered the information was right on.

   We actually store memories and emotions in our hearts. There are numerous cases of patients who have had heart trauma or a heart replacement who experienced a change in their personalities. So know the heart is more than just a muscle that pumps blood. It's a treasure chest of intelligence and wisdom that definitely needs to be a part of the decision-making process.

2. **Your Gut** is called "the second brain." Yep, the gut has a significant amount of neurons that communicate directly with the brain. Sometimes we just have a "gut feeling" about something and our brain can't figure out why. But learn to listen to those gut-based instincts your body has developed over millions of years of evolution. All the most successful people do.

The idea here is to use all the tools at your disposal. Don't discount your gut instincts because something looks great on paper. Try and understand what your gut is telling you. Believe me, when I've rejected my gut instincts I've made atrociously bad decisions.

I highly recommend using these three separate intelligences in your body, asking:
1. What does my head say?
2. What does my heart say?
3. What does my gut say?

Then pay close attention to the responses. It's the winning trifecta.

The decision-making process in a nutshell:

Step 1:
Decide "What is the outcome I most desire?
Describe it in detail.

Step 2:
What assumptions need to be converted to facts?
What are the facts?
What resources are available?

Step 3:

How does this decision align with my Top 5 Values?

Will any higher values be sacrificed for a lower value?

Step 4:

Slow down.

Recharge with energy, water, and rest.

Visualize the results of your potential options

(Always aim to come up with at least three options where possible. This forces you to keep asking yourself "What else could I do?")

Step 5:

Ask: What does my brain tell me?

Ask: What does my heart tell me?

Ask: What does my gut tell me?

This is a simple process. Please realize that decision-making is not an exact science and it's not infallible. Plus, life can have other ideas for us. For the most important decisions in life, it's highly beneficial to get expert advice from a coach, counselor, therapist, consultant, or other appropriate professional(s). Sometimes they will see what you can't.

And finally …

Play in the land of *meaningful*

Making decisions is hard work. It uses a lot of brain energy and is mentally and physically fatiguing. So when it comes to decision-making I only want to be dealing with the stuff that really matters. (This also relates to time management.)

The first thing I always ask when something comes up in my life is: "Is this opportunity or request ESSENTIAL or DESIRABLE?" Even when I'm checking emails, my first question with each one is, "Will this be a drain on my time and brainpower?" If yes, I hit delete. Next I ask: "Is this my responsibility?" If the answer is "no," I hit delete.

We all have to make a huge number of decisions, big and small, each and every day. They all take energy and time. So it helps to reduce the amount of decisions we need to make.

Learn from bad decisions

When I look at my poor decisions and my clients' less than optimum choices, I find the biggest mistakes are:
1. Rushing the process
2. Not getting clear on the facts
3. Listening to poor advice
4. Not tapping into all our external resources
5. Not tapping into all our internal resources (our brains, hearts and guts)
6. Being emotionally reactive as opposed to consciously responsive
7. Being influenced by others opinions
8. Trying to arrive at a perfect outcome
9. Not having the skills required to execute the course of action
10. Making decisions based on what you think other people will think of you

Better decisions = better results. I hope these points help you to become more aware and effective in your own decision-making process.

CHAPTER 27
Conclusion

I wrote this book to clarify what leads us to experience success more deeply in our lives and to explore the often-distorted perception that having lots of money and possessions will make us feel more successful.

A lot of people have a lot of money, a lot of possessions, a big company and the word "founder" or the initials CEO on their business cards. But are they happy? Do they feel deep success at every level of their being? In 2009, Adolf Merckle, a German businessman, committed suicide because his net worth had dropped down to US$6 Billion. Perhaps there was more going on for Merckle than just numbers changing on his balance sheet. But perhaps not.

How many tycoons committed suicide during last century's Great Depression?

As Madonna made clear a few decades ago, we live in a material world. We also live in a highly reductionist world, where everything from medicine to mental health to consumerism is driven by the desire to identify the singular thing(s) responsible for the whole result. We look at an apple and reduce it to its Vitamin C content and believe that's what makes it healthy as opposed to the whole apple with its flavorful symphony of macro and micro-nutrients. We go for the pill and throw the apple away.

We've done the same thing with success.

Only when we preface it with the word *authentic* do we start to uncover the interrelated components that are necessary for us to feel deeply successful and happy on a consistent basis. In the process we start to see that money is only one of the many by-products of working to achieve our goals—and that pursuing goals aligned with our purpose and values—pursuing goals that are good for us, good for others, and good for the greater good bring us to an entirely different level of experience in life. A higher, more deeply rewarding experience.

I hope you've found many takeaways in this book—that you've found beneficial strategies that will get your life moving forward—that you've gained not only insights but picked up some practical tools and strategies you can apply to evolve your life, your business, and the levels of joy, health and connection you are currently experiencing.

As an author, it can be a challenge to decide what the most impactful parting words might be for readers. What can I say that will resonate most profoundly—so much so it will launch them into their personal transformation and evolution? Here's what comes to mind for me.

Knowledge does not become wisdom until it has been consciously applied and experienced. I encourage you to take the specific actions suggested in this book and then learn from them. If you haven't done all the exercises, figuring you'll get back to them—get back to them.

You have an incredible amount of potential within you that has yet to be fully expressed. You have the desire to feel more successful, joyful, happy, and fulfilled in life. You want to make a difference in the lives of others.

And you can do it.

Don't allow yourself to be seduced into the idea that success is for someone else. Everything you need is within you right now. Don't compare yourself to others you believe are more successful than you. Trust me, they have their own inner challenges.

Don't measure your success using society's scorecard.

Measure your success by the quality of the relationships you have in your life. Measure your success by the number of times you smile or laugh each day. Measure your success by the connection you feel with yourself and this thing called life.

Measure your success by the meaning you bring to the smallest things you do. Measure your success by the fact that you are courageous enough to show up as your imperfect perfect self. Measure your success by the level of vitality you have coursing through your body. Measure your success by how daring you are when it comes to trying new things that cause you to grow and evolve. And lastly, measure yourself by the confidence you feel in your ability to generate more money if and when you need it.

If these are the standards by which you measure yourself, I can assure you that you will feel successful—not as a fleeting emotion, but as a consistent joyous condition flowing from the very core of your being.

This is the kind of success I desire for you.

Thank you for allowing me to be your guide.

CHAPTER 28

Recommended Resources

CONTINUING YOUR JOURNEY TO AUTHENTIC SUCCESS

I am SO very grateful you joined me on this journey behind the scenes of success and I look forward to serving you and crossing paths with you in the weeks, months and years to come.

If you want to fire some questions my way, or just reach out and say 'hi,' just drop into my Carl Massy Facebook Page and connect up. I would love to hear from you and love to hear what you learned reading this book.

You can also track me down, sign up for my fortnightly newsletter and get some great free resources at www.carlmassy.com.

Also, I would be SO GRATEFUL (really I would), if you would do me the honour of leaving a comment on Amazon or Goodreads or the likes, to let me (and others know) what you thought of this book. It's through your support that I can continue to serve by taking my message that 'feeling successful requires us to look beyond societies fixation on money' to a broader audience.

If you want to continue your journey to authentic success and evolve into the greatest version of yourself possible, I would love to continue being your guide. Whether that is 1-on-1 as your Coach, or in workshops, courses and retreats I am involved with just check out www.carlmassy.com for more details.

High Performance Coaching

I love working 1-on-1 with a select number of people each year that are ready, willing, and committed to taking their life up to a whole new level. I know you are not tapping into your full potential and we have not seen the best of you yet. If you are ready to go to work with me to help to make your greatest desires manifest and feel successful in your bones, then get in touch with me and let's get the conversation started.

The Practice (Bali Yoga Centre)

If you ever needed an excuse to come to Bali, here is a great one. Come and join me and The Practice team for some awesome yoga, cool presentations, transformative workshops and life changing courses. At The Practice we are about the practice of deep, mindful and conscious yoga; with a focus on not only what you do on the mat, but also how it helps you to become a better and more evolved human being off the mat. I would love to meet you in person there one day.

Check out www.thepracticebali.com to find out more.

The 30-Day Challenge

This unique 6-week coaching program is life changing. It consists of online and offline coaching tailored to your individual needs, PLUS 6 powerful one-on-one weekly coaching sessions which will teach you not only the foundational elements of health and happiness, but also techniques to develop the greatest habits of happiness, health, vitality, creativity, productivity and success. If you want to upgrade the course of your life, overcome challenges, achieve your biggest goals, and love the way you feel on a daily basis, this program is the game changer for you.

Check out www.carlmassy.com/30-day-challenge for all the details.

CHAPTER 29
Recommended Reading

THE BRAIN
David Rock, *Your Brain at Work*
Dr Joe Dispenza, *Evolve Your Brain*
John Medina, PhD, *Brain Rules*

EMPOWERMENT
David Hawkins, *Power Vs Force*
Dr Joe Dispenza, *Breaking the Habit of Being Yourself*
Steven Kotler, *The Rise of Superman*

ENTREPRENEURIAL
Darren Hardy, *The Entrepreneur Roller Coaster*
Simon Sinek, *Start with Why*
Steven Pressfield, *The War of Art*

GENERAL HEALTH
Dr Dean Ornish, *Dr Dean Ornish's Program for Reversing Heart Disease*

Deepak Chopra MD, *Ageless Body, Timeless Mind*
Jim Loehr and Tony Schwartz, *The Power of Full Engagement*

HAPPINESS
Byron Katie, *Loving What Is*
Martin Seligman, *Flourishing*
Tal Ben-Shahar, *Happier*

MEDITATION
Eknath Easwaran, *Conquest of Mind*
Jon Kabat-Zinn, *Wherever You Go There You Are*
Matthieu Ricard, *Why Meditate?*

METAPHYSICAL
Cate Montana, *The E-word*
Deepak Chopra, *The Seven Spiritual Laws of Success*
Eckhart Tolle, *A New Earth*

THE MIND-BODY CONNECTION
Dr Joe Dispenza, *You Are The Placebo*
Dr Bruce Lipton, *The Biology of Belief*
Dr Darren Weissman, *The Power of Infinite Love and Gratitude*

PERSONAL DEVELOPMENT
Brene Brown, *Daring Greatly*
Carol Dweck, *Mindset*
Don Miguel Ruiz, *The Four Agreements*

NUTRITION
Dr Colin T Campbell, *The China Study*
Gene Stone, *Forks over Knives*
Dr Joel Fuhrman, MD, *Eat To Live*

WEALTH
Dean Graziosi, *Millionaire Success Habits*
M J DeMarco, *The Millionaire Fastlane*
Tony Robbins, *Money*

Acknowledgements

There are very specific people who did very specific things to get this book across the line, and then there are all the other people in my life that create the environment that allowed this book to be created.

The person most instrumental in bringing this book into physical form is my partner Ferry Tan, who not only does the cover work, book layout, and final packaging, but she keeps me on track. Without her, there might be a whole lot more meandering and moving of milestones.

My editor Cate Montana is always a part of making what I think is a great book, that much better. And this time she did it while managing the book launch of her very awesome book, *'The E-Word: Ego, Enlightenment and other Essentials'*. Thanks for making space for me Cate.

My business partners at *The Practice* yoga centre in Bali – Octavio Salvado and Rob Dubois – are instrumental in my life for their inspiration, feedback, and also an opportunity to practice this thing called 'authentic success'. Together we get to work on what it means to be authentically successful, and learn and grow as we go.

A big shout out to my dad, who is one of my greatest fans and is happy to put up his hand when it comes to the not-so-fun jobs like 'proof reading'. Love the support and encouragement dad. Plus mum for just loving me even when I am being a less than ideal version of myself. It's always great to have that unconditional love to lean on.

I have had numerous teachers over the years and the joy of reading and learning from 100's of authors who have taken the time to put their ideas into words, for me and others to digest. Some of my favourite teachers include Joe Dispenza, Bruce Lipton, Darren Weissman, Tony Robbins, and Brene Brown. Then there are colleagues and friends who keep you honest and provide a sounding board that is essential in doing great work. So thank you.

Finally, I learn and grow with every conversation I have with every client of mine. They provide me insights, ideas, real-life experiences and a reminder of what I might have forgotten myself. So to every client – past and present – I am deeply grateful for you allowing me to do what I do, to be a part of your evolution and for supporting me along the way.

Made in the USA
Charleston, SC
12 February 2017